Bilge Huschebeck

The Impact of the
EU-General Data Protection Regulation
on Facebook and Google

Huschebeck, Bilge: The Impact of the EU-General Data Protection Regulation on Facebook and Google, Hamburg, Bachelor + Master Publishing 2020
Originaltitel der Abschlussarbeit: The Impact of the EU-General Data Protection Regulation on Facebook and Google

Buch-ISBN: 978-3-95993-088-8
PDF-eBook-ISBN: 978-3-95993-588-3
Druck/Herstellung: Bachelor + Master Publishing, Hamburg, 2020
Zugl. Leibniz Universität Hannover, Hannover, Deutschland, Masterarbeit, September 2019

Bibliografische Information der Deutschen Nationalbibliothek:
Die Deutsche Nationalbibliothek verzeichnet diese Publikation in der Deutschen Nationalbibliografie; detaillierte bibliografische Daten sind im Internet über http://dnb.d-nb.de abrufbar.

© Bachelor + Master Publishing, Imprint der Bedey Media GmbH
Hermannstal 119k, 22119 Hamburg
http://www.bachelor-master-publishing.de, Hamburg 2020
Printed in Germany

Table of contents

Abbreviations

(National) Data Protection Authorities	DPAs
Article 29 Working Party	WP29
Data Protection Directive	DPD
E-Privacy Directive	EPD
European Court of Human Right	ECtHR
European Court of Justice	ECJ / CJEU
European Data Protection Board	EDPB
Federal Trade Commission	FTC
General Data Protection Regulation	GDPR

1   Introduction

Google and Facebook are among the most active and effective companies when it comes to collecting and processing personal data. The core of their business activities is highly dependent on personal data collected to be used for online behavioural advertising. However, the privacy incidents and the revealed activities of these companies regarding unlawful data collection, processing and sharing with 3rd parties without valid consent of the users, triggered some privacy concerns of the individuals and accordingly series of actions by the DPAs. Thus, complying with the GDPR became important for companies not only to prevent the financial loss based on the imposed fines but also to protect their reputation for respecting users' privacy. However, it is still open to discussion whether data subjects have any control over their data in scope of the principles and rights regulated under the GDPR.

It has been a while since the German Federal Constitutional Court interpreted privacy as informational self-determination in 1983, as *"the capacity of the individual to determine in principle the disclosure and use of his/her personal data".* [1] However, with the increasing use of information technologies, the imbalance of power escalated between the data subjects and controllers. Since collecting and processing vast amounts of data enabled the data controllers to *"... take decisions about individual subjects on the basis of these collected and processed personal information without allowing for any possibility for the data subjects to know exactly which data would be used, for which purposes, for which duration and overall without control... ".* [2] Accordingly, data protection regulations and mechanisms were developed, the final form of the modern data privacy legislation today is the General Data Protection Regulation(GDPR) in the EU. [3] Still there are some scholars arguing that the users are solely responsible for their privacy, since the users are the ones freely entering into agreements and

---

[1]   BVerfGE 65, 1 – Volkszählung Urteil des Ersten Senats vom 15. Dezember 1983 auf die mündliche Verhandlung vom 18. und 19. Oktober 1983 – 1 BvR 209, 269, 362, 420, 440, 484/83 in den Verfahren über die Verfassungsbeschwerden. (15.12.1983)

[2] Rouvroy, Antoinette, and Yves Poullet. "The Right to Informational Self-determination and the Value of Self-development. Reassessing the Importance of Privacy for Democracy." In Reinventing Data Protection? (2009), p. 68.

[3] "Regulation (EU) 2016/679 of The European Parliament and of The Council on the protection of natural persons with regard to the processing of personal data and on the free movement of such data, and repealing Directive 95/46/EC (General Data Protection Regulation), OJ L. 119/1, 4.5.2016."

contracts with the service providers and companies for the protection of their data.[4] However, as mentioned above the imbalance between the controllers and data subjects necessitated the intervention of the governments to protect the rights of the data subjects. Even though privacy issues have been raised in the US and European Union lately and legal instruments have been implemented to regulate the collecting and processing of personal data in order to protect data subjects' rights, data breaches and unlawful personal data collections happen more and more on a daily basis.

The key challenge now is whether the GDPR impacts the business model of Facebook and Google, since the scandal of Cambridge Analytica revealed that "transparency" has no meaning in today's online market, where individuals' data is the currency. Even though GDPR provides some fundamental rights for the data subjects, it could be argued that the data subjects have no effective control over their data in the online market in practice. Therefore, it is necessary to analyse within the scope of this book, whether GDPR sets adequate safeguards regarding the data subjects' rights, regarding data owners' consent, purpose limitation principle and the right to be informed. It is also important to analyse whether Google and Facebook meet the requirements of the GDPR in practice. Thus, the aim of this book is to illuminate the interaction of legislative decree and business practices of Facebook and Google. However, this book does not intend to cover every single aspect of the GDPR and practices of Facebook and Google.

1.1   Research Question

The aim of the book is to answer following question:

- Do Google and Facebook sufficiently comply with the current data protection law in the EU regarding the data subjects' rights and control over their data?

---

[4] Smith, H. Jeff, "Information Privacy and its Management," MIS Quarterly Executive: Vol. 3: Issue 4, Article 6 (2008) p. 201.

1.2   Structure

In order to answer the research questions, a general information regarding the business models of Facebook and Google will be provided in Chapter 2. This Chapter aims to provide a general overview of the business activities of Facebook and Google, and demonstrates the dominance of these companies in the online market. The relevant legal framework will be examined in Chapter 3, in an attempt to review the related provisions of the GDPR to this book generally before implementing it to practices of Google and Facebook. As the core business of Google and Facebook are online behavioural advertising, Chapter 4, provides a general information how the automated decision-making and profiling are regulated under the GDPR. Further, the legal frameworks for cookies are provided to analyse cookie policies of Google and Facebook, since the cookies are part of the main tracking methods for these companies. Since both companies are US-based, a general information on the international transfers of the personal data are provided in the Chapter 5 to assess later on, whether an adequate level of protection is provided for the personal data regarding the data flows between the company subsidiaries taking place in US and EU. Finally, to analyse if Google and Facebook comply with the GDPR on certain aspects, the privacy policies of companies will be assessed on the scope of general principles of the GDPR, consent and other legal grounds for processing and certain data subjects' rights. To determine whether the privacy policies meet the reality to comply with the GDPR regarding data subjects' rights, selected enforcements by the DPAs and important case decisions by the CJEU concerning Google and Facebook along with the Cambridge Analytica scandal will be further examined.

It should be noted that this book does not aim to cover every aspect of the GDPR and practices of Google and Facebook. Therefore, only selected aspects of the GDPR along with cases will be examined to find out whether data subjects have any control over their data.

2 Business Models of Facebook and Google

2.1 Facebook

Facebook is a social networking service launched in 2003 and founded by March Zuckerberg, Eduardo Saverin, Andrew McCollum, Dustin Moskovitz and Chris Huges. Today, Facebook, Inc. is one of the biggest tech companies competing with Google, Amazon and Apple. Facebook, Inc. has various products including Facebook, Instagram, Messenger, WhatsApp and Occulus which are used for collecting data, creating targeted advertisements and profiles and replacements of the adds based on the collected personal data.[5]

Facebook's core business model is selling advertising placements to marketers. Almost all of the revenue (over 98%) is maintained by targeted advertising.[6] Facebook Ads enable the marketers to reach targeted induvial or groups based on different factors including age, gender, location, interests and behaviours.[7] The ads purchased by marketers can appear simultaneously on Facebook, Instagram, Messenger and third-party applications and websites. Meanwhile, Facebook invests in other consumer hardware products, connectivity efforts, AI and augmented reality for long-term purposes of product development.[8] Daily active users of Facebook worldwide are 1,562 million and in Europe 286 million by on average by the end of March 31, 2019.[9]

2.2 Google

Google is an American based company founded by Larry Page and Serge Brin in 1998 specialised in internet services and products including online advertising technologies, cloud

---

[5] The term Facebook is used as Facebook, Inc. including the products mentioned above.

[6] United States Securities and Exchange Commission Form 10-K, "Annual Report of Facebook, Inc." (For the fiscal year ended 31.12.2018), Available at:
https://www.sec.gov/Archives/edgar/data/1326801/000132680119000009/fb-12312018x10k.htm (Accessed: 11.09.2019), p.42.

[7] Ibid., p. 5.

[8] Ibid.

[9] United States Securities and Exchange Commission, Form 10-Q, "Quarterly Report of Facebook, Inc." (For the quarterly period ended 31.03.2019), Available at:
https://www.sec.gov/Archives/edgar/data/1326801/000132680119000037/fb-03312019x10q.htm. (Accessed: 11.09.2019), p. 26.

computing, search engine, software and hardware. The Alphabet Inc, mother company of Google, encompasses from self-driving cars to GoogleCloud to internet-beaming hot air balloons.[10] The company structure of the Google is quite complicated since the company has many subsidiaries with various business activities.

The core products and platforms of Google includes Chrome, Gmail, Google Drive, Google Search, Youtube, Google Maps and Google Play, GoogleCloud and Android. Each one of these products or platforms have over one billion monthly active users. The income of the Google is mostly based on performance and brand advertising along with other sources of income.[11] Performance advertising creates and delivers relevant ads that users will click on and brand advertising allows brand advertisers to deliver digital videos and other types of ads to specific target group for their marketing campaigns.[12]

2.3   Controller or not?

The term controller is defined as " *the natural or legal person, public authority, agency or other body which, alone or jointly with others, determines the purposes and means of the processing of personal data; where the purposes and means of such processing are determined by Union or Member State law, the controller or the specific criteria for its nomination may be provided for by Union or Member State law*" in the GDPR.[13]

Some scholars are of the view that the definition is too general and under this definition; individuals, who provide content and data about themselves or others in the social media platforms such as Facebook could also be considered as "controller".[14] However, it is hard to accept that "providing data" as "data processing" under the GDPR. As ruled in the *Wirtschaftsakademie* case *"... the mere fact of making use of a social network such as Face-*

---

[10] Alphabet Inc., Available at: https://abc.xyz (Accessed: 11.09.2019)

[11] United States Securities and Exchange Commission, Form 10-Q, "Annual Report of Alphabet Inc. " (For the fiscal year ended 31.12.2018). Available at: https://www.sec.gov/Archives/edgar/data/1652044/000165204419000004/goog10-kq42018.htm#s6C1DB95EDB3C5C7998B5E96D339C677B (Accessed: 11.09.2019), p. 4.

[12] Ibid.

[13] GDPR, Art. 4(7).

[14] Wong, Rebecca," Social Networking: Anybody is a Data Controller", (2009), p. 142.

book does not make a Facebook user a controller jointly responsible for the processing of personal data by that network... ".[15]

The roles of Facebook and Google regarding data processing will be determined based on the GDPR and case-law of the ECJ. The ECJ interprets the term "controller" broadly in its case law to secure effective and complete protection of data subjects.

In Case Google Spain the Court considered an operator of a search engine as a controller.[16] The court mentioned that the activities of the search engine are liable to affect significantly and additionally the fundamental rights to privacy and to the protection of personal data, compared to publishers of websites. As a result, Google, as the operator of the search engine, determining the purposes and means of that activity must ensure to meet the requirements of the GDPR.[17]

The Court followed its previous ruling in the case of Facebook.[18] Since Wirtschaftsakademie gives Facebook the opportunity to place cookies on the devices of a person visiting the fan page, whether or not that person has a Facebook account, Wirtschaftsakademie is jointly responsible with Facebook Ireland Ltd.[19] Thus, Wirtschaftsakademie can be considered as a joint controller.

Lately, the Court ruled that operator of a website "*that embeds on that website a social plugin causing the browser of a visitor to that website to request content from the provider of that plugin and transmit to that provider the personal data of the visitor*" can be considered as controller.[20] According to the Court, even though the Fashion ID had no access to the personal data collected and transmitted to the Facebook, they are considered as joint controllers since they determine the means and purposes of the processing together.[21]

---

[15] Unabhängiges Landeszentrum für Datenschutz Schleswig-Holstein v. Wirtschaftsakademie Schleswig-Holstein GmbH, C-210/16 (CJEU, 5 June 2018), para. 35.

[16] Google Spain SL, Google Inc. v. Agencia Española de Protección de Datos (AEPD), Mario Costeja González, C-131/12 (CJEU, 13 May 2014), para. 32 and 33.

[17] Ibid.

[18] Unabhängiges Landeszentrum für Datenschutz Schleswig-Holstein v. Wirtschaftsakademie Schleswig-Holstein GmbH, C-210/16 (CJEU, 5 June 2018)

[19] Ibid., p. 35, 39, 40 and 42.

[20] Fashion ID GmbH & Co. KG v. Verbraucherzentrale NRW eV, C-40/17 (CJEU, 29 July 2019), para.64.

[21] Ibid., para.84.

Finally, the activities of Google as a search engine operator are accepted as data processing under GDPR since Google collects, retrieves, organises and stores the personal data on its servers.[22] Moreover, not only is Facebook considered as controller under the GDPR but also the users of its products determining the purposes and means of the processing are considered as joint controllers.

---

[22] Google Spain Case, C-131/12, para. 28.

3   Basics of the GDPR to Collect and Process Personal Data

3.1   Some of the General Principles of the GDPR

Principles in general are abstractions determinate the essence and the basis of a set of legal rules.[23] General principles of data processing in the EU are mostly regulated under Art. 5 of the GDPR. These principles set out not only obligations for businesses and organizations which collect, process and store personal data, but also rights for the data subjects. The principles are also functioning as guiding standards when interpreting the legislation.

3.1.1   Fair and Lawful Processing

One of the primary principles of the data protection law are fair and lawful processing regulated under Art. 5(1)(a) of the GDPR. The term "fairness" is quite abstract in the GDPR. Thus, it is difficult to define. It could however be said that it embraces some of the fundamental principles such as transparency, purpose limitation and proportionality.

For data processing to be lawful, it must be based on consent or one of the other legitimate grounds provided in the Article 6 (1) of the GDPR. Principle of fairness requires the data processing to be done in a fair manner. In that sense, the controller needs to ensure the data subjects that there are no unforeseeable negative effects caused by data processing and inform them about the potential risks.[24] Moreover, the interest and the reasonable expectations of the data subjects need to be considered by the controller. Therefore, balance and proportionality are integral part of fairness.[25] This also includes for the controller to be acting within the frame of the wishes of the data subject as much as possible. Especially when the data subject's consent forms the legal basis of the data processing.[26] In British Gas Trading Case, the Tribunal ruled that individuals should be informed of any non-specific purpose for processing

---

[23] Lee A. Bygrave, *Data privacy law : an international perspective* (Oxford: Oxford University Press, 2014), p. 145.

[24] European Union Agency for Fundamental Rights and Council of Europe, "Handbook on European data protection law", (2018), p. 118.

[25] Bygrave, *Data privacy law : an international perspective*, p. 146.

[26] K.H. and Others v. Slovakia No. 32881/04, (ECtHR, 28 April 2009), para 50.

at the time they enter into the relationship with the controller. Also, wider uses of the data without the consent of the data subject has been found to be unfair.[27]

The principle could also be interpreted as a protection from abuse of the controllers of their monopoly position, as well as direct data collection from the data subjects, and not from third parties.[28]

3.1.2 Transparency

Transparency principle is regulated under Art. 5(1)(a) of the GDPR and it requires the personal data relating to natural persons to be transparent about how the data are *"collected, used, consulted or otherwise processed and to what extent the personal data are or will be processed."*[29] In that sense, the identity of the controller, purposes of the processing, information necessary for the natural persons to use their right to obtain confirmation and communication of personal data concerning them, the risks, rules, safeguards and rights regarding the processing of personal data and how to exercise their rights in relation to such processing must be provided by the controller.[30] Moreover, the principle of transparency requires that the information addressed to the public or data subject to be *"concise, easily accessible and easy to understand, and that clear and plain language"*.[31] It is particularly important for data subjects to know *"by whom and for what purpose personal data relating to him or her are being collected"*.[32]

Transparency principle is also crucial for the usage of artificial intelligence (AI) and automated decision-making processes, since the GDPR requires the controllers to provide the grounds for the decision made by the AI.[33] For instance, in the case of online behavioural advertising, the controller is responsible for providing information to the users, on what grounds a specific advertisement is shown to the specific user. However, there are technical challenges to provide such information because of the vast amount of data collection; such as the black-box

---

[27] British Gas Trading Limited vs. The Data Protection Register, (UK Data Protection Tribunal, March 1997).

[28] Bygrave, *Data privacy law : an international perspective*, p. 147.

[29] GDPR, Recital 39.

[30] Ibid.

[31] GDPR, Recital 58.

[32] Ibid.

[33] GDPR, Art. 12.

issue.[34] It can be said that the black-box issue is one of the technically weak points regarding to comply with the principle of transparency in the GDPR so far. In case of the companies such as Facebook and Google, providing the necessities of the principle of transparency might help to increase the productivity for the advertisers using their Ads services. Since an explanation will be given by the AI, the reason why it shows a specific advertisement to a specific person on what bases, will be clear.

3.1.3   Purpose Specification and Limitation Principle

This principle is manifested in GDPR Art. 5(1)(b) and DPD Art 6(1)(b) as one of the core principles of data privacy and protection. It the personal data to be collected for "*specified, explicit and legitimate purposes and the data is not further processed in a manner that is incompatible with those purposes.*"[35] The principle is connected with the transparency, consent and user control as well as the predictability.[36]

Even though the purpose limitation principle is one of the most important principles in the GDPR, the principle is not especially significant in the case law. For instance, ECtHR stated in the S. and Marper v. United Kingdom case:[37]

> "*The domestic law should notably ensure that such data are relevant and not excessive in relation to the purposes for which they are stored; and preserved in a form which permits identification of the data subjects for no longer than is required for the purpose for which those data are stored.*"

There are some other related case law by the ECtHR[38], but none of the judgements brings specific explanation to the principle.

According to the Bygrave, purpose limitation principle can be divided into three separate principles:[39]

---

[34] See Zednik, Carlos. "Solving the Black Box Problem: A Normative Framework for Explainable Artificial Intelligence." (2019), p.3.

[35] GDPR, Art. 5(1)(b)

[36] Article 29 Working Party (2013), Opinion 3/2013 on purpose limitation, WP 203, 2 April 2013.

[37] S. and Marper v. the United Kingdom, No. 30562/04 30566/04 (ECtHR, 2008), para.103.

[38] Such as Rotaru v. Romania No. 28341/95 (ECtHR, 2000) and Amann v. Switzerland, No. 27798/95, (ECtHR 2000).

"(1) the purposes for which data is collected shall be defined and made explicit;

(2) these purposes shall be lawful or legitimate;

(3) the purposes for which the data is further processed shall not be incompati-

ble with the purposes for which the data is originally collected."

The term "incompatible" is especially important to define the scope of the processing and whether it is lawful. According to the recital 50 of the GDPR reasonable expectations of the data subjects must also be taken into account by the controller.

3.1.4   Data Minimisation Principle

According to the Art. 5(1)(c) of the GDPR, personal data that has been collected or processed should be *"adequate, relevant and limited to what is necessary in relation to the purposes for which they are processed"*.[40] Data minimisation principle is also closely related with the storage limitation, purpose limitation and proportionality principles as well as data privacy by design and default.[41] The principle basically limits the amount of personal data collected regarding how necessary the personal data is to achieve the purposes of the processing. Moreover, the principle covers the anonymisation of personal data, when it is not necessary anymore to keep the personal data for the specific purposes it has been collected.[42] In other words, if it is possible to avoid collecting personal data at all, means of anonymisation and pseudonymisation, data minimisation principle requires to use these measures to reduce personal data. Privacy Enhancing Technologies (PETs) can be used in scope of Art 25 of the GDPR to eliminate or reduce the personal data in the processing or prevent unnecessary personal data at the first place.

Even though the principle largely depends on "necessity" criteria, it is not defined in the GDPR. According to Bygrave, the criterion might be developed regarding the case law on ECHR Art. 8(2), by applying pressing social or commercial need and proportionality criteria. [43] However, CJEU ruled that the "necessary" is a concept with its own independent meaning

---

[39] Bygrave, *Data privacy law : an international perspective*, p. 155.

[40] GDPR, Art. 5(1)(c) and Modernised Convention 108, Art. 5 (4) (c).

[41] GDPR, Arts. 5(1)(c) and (e), 6(1), 9(1), 11, 25.

[42] GDPR, Art. 11 and 25.

[43] Bygrave, L.A. "Data Protection Law: Approaching Its Rationale, Logic and Limits." Journal of Information, Law & Technology 1 (2002): Journal of Information, Law & Technology Vol.1(2002), p. 341.

"and which must be interpreted in a manner which fully reflects the objective of that directive..." Further, the necessity criterion in DPD Art. 7(e) is met if the processing leads to enhanced effectiveness meaning that "necessary" not meaning indispensable.[44]

3.1.5   Storage Limitation

The storage limitation principle refers to deletion of personal data or anonymisation of the data as soon as the data are no longer necessary for the purposes for which they were collected.[45] The principle applies only to the data that allows the identification of the data subjects. Moreover, the retention period is determined according to the type of personal data and purposes for the data collection. Data storage for public interest, scientific or historical purposes, or for statistical use, may be for longer periods.[46]

However, certain period of time for retention of the personal data is not enacted in the legislation. Accordingly, on the grounds of uncertain retention period (from six months up to two years) and no existence of objective criteria provided in the legislation, the CJEU invalidated the Data Retention Directive.[47] The court also ruled in the *Tele2* case that: "*the national legislation must be based on objective evidence which makes it possible to identify a public whose data is likely to reveal a link, at least an indirect one, with serious criminal offences, and to contribute in one way or another to fighting serious crime or to preventing a serious risk to public security. Such limits may be set by using a geographical criterion where the competent national authorities consider, on the basis of objective evidence, that there exists, in one or more geographical areas, a high risk of preparation for or commission of such offences".[48]*

Currently, the uncertainty for the retention periods remains, since the national legislations fail to set objective criteria.

---

[44] Heinz Huber v. Bundesrepublik Deutschland [GC], C-524/06, (CJEU, 2008), para. 62-66.

[45] GDPR, Art. 5(1)(e).

[46] Ibid.

[47] Joined cases Digital Rights Ireland Ltd v. Minister for Communications, Marine and Natural Resources and Others and Kärntner Landesregierung and Others, C-293/12 and C-594/12, (CJEU, 2014).

[48] Joined Cases Tele2 Sverige AB v. Postoch telestyrelsen, and Secretary of State for the Home Department, C-203/15 and C-698/15, (CJEU, 21.12.2016), para.111.

3.1.6   Disclosure Limitation

Principle of disclosure limitation is not included in the GDPR nor in the DPD as a separate principle. However, it can be found in the OECD Guidelines under the name of "use limitation" principle.[49] The principle indicates that no disclosure of personal data, except the cases that a valid consent from the data subject is obtained for the disclosure or the disclosure of the data is necessary by the authority of law.[50]

3.2   Legal Grounds to Collect the Data

Article 6 of the GDPR sets out an exhaustive and restrictive list of cases in which the processing of personal data considered as lawful.[51] Lawful grounds for processing data consists of; consent of the data subject, data processing is necessary for the performance of a contract, processing is necessary for compliance with a legal obligation of the controller, vital interests of data subject or another natural person. Further processing is necessary for the performance of a task carried out in the public interest, and is based on the legitimate interest of controllers or third parties with the exception that interests are not overridden by the interests or the fundamental rights of the data subjects. As "consent" is one of the most common legal grounds in practice, especially in cases of Facebook and Google, it is of particularly importance under this section. Since, legitimate interest of the controller for direct marketing purposes is another most used legal ground for practices of Google and Facebook, it will be analysed under this section. However it is relevant, since the legal ground of necessity to conduct a contract varies to specific cases, it will be analysed regarding the specific cases of Facebook and Google under the privacy policy section.

3.2.1   Consent

Consent is one of the most used legal grounds for processing personal data in general, especially in cases of Google and Facebook. The concept of consent under EU law as a legal

---

[49] OECD Guidelines on data protection (2013) – Guidelines Governing the Protection of Privacy and Transborder Flows of Personal Data, (Adopted 23.9.1980). Available at: http://www.oecd.org/sti/ieconomy/2013-oecd-privacy-guidelines.pdf

[50] Ibid., p. 14.

[51] GDPR, Art. 6.

ground for data processing is established under Art. 6 of the GDPR and Art. 8 of the Charter. Consent is defined as *"any freely given, specific, informed and unambiguous indication of the data subject's wishes by which he or she, by a statement or by a clear affirmative action, signifies agreement to the processing of personal data relating to him or her"* in the GDPR.[52] The conditions of consent are regulated under Art. 7 of the GDPR and requires the controller to be able to demonstrate if the consent is given.[53] Moreover, the request for consent must be *"clearly distinguishable from the other matters, in an intelligible and easily accessible form, using clear and plain language"*, otherwise it is not binding for the data subject.[54] Data subjects can withdraw their consent any time and the procedure of withdrawal must be easy.[55] Even though, it is mentioned that the terms, for which consent is required, should not be unfair, it could be argued how it takes place in practice.[56] For consent to be valid four elements needs be provided; freely given, informed, specific and unambiguous.

3.2.1.1   Freely given

Consent of the data subject must *"represent the free expression of an intentional choice"* according to the CoE framework of Modernised Convention 108.[57] In that sense, data subject must be able to exercise a real choice without the risk of deception, intimidation, coercion or significant negative consequences in case that data subject does not consent.[58]For consent to be freely given, there must be no clear imbalance between the controller and data subject.[59] Freely given consent excludes the cases when it is not possible to give separate consent to different personal data processing operations.[60]

---

[52] GDPR, Art. 4(11).

[53] GDPR, Art. 7(1).

[54] GDPR, Art. 7(2).

[55] GDPR, Art. 7(3).

[56] GDPR, Recital 42.

[57] Explanatory Report of Modernised Convention 108, para. 42.

[58] Article 29 Working Party (2011), Opinion 15/2011 on the notion of consent, WP 187, Brussels, 13 July 2011, p. 12.

[59] GDPR, Recital 43.

[60] Ibid.

In cases in which the only way to obtain goods or services goes through disclosing personal data to the controller or further on to the third parties, consent of data subject to disclose data, which is not necessary for the contract, cannot be considered as a free decision.[61]

3.2.1.2 Informed

Sufficient information about personal data processing must be provided to the data subject. In scope of informed consent, it is required that *"the data subject should be aware at least of the identity of the controller and the purposes of the processing for which the personal data are intended."*[62] Moreover, the information about the type of the data being collected and used, the existence of the right to withdraw consent, information regarding usage of data for automated decision-making if relevant and finally possible risks of data transfers in cases that absence of an adequacy decision and appropriate safeguards (GDPR, Art. 46) must be provided to the data subjects.[63] The quality of information should also be taken into account by the controller, especially regarding the used language to be understandable and availability of the information by the users.[64]

3.2.1.3 Specific

Consent needs to be specific to the purpose(s) of the processing in order to be valid. In the case that processing has multiple purposes, consent should be given for all of them.[65] The controller needs to apply following to comply with the element of "specific" according to the WP29:[66]

> *"1. Purpose specification as a safeguard against function creep,*
>
> *2. Granularity in consent requests, and*

---

[61] GDPR, Art. 7(4).

[62] Ibid.

[63] Article 29 Working Party, Guidelines on consent under Regulation 2016/679, WP259 rev.01, Brussels, 10.04.2018, p. 13.

[64] Article 29 Working Party (2011), Opinion 15/2011 on the definition of consent, WP187, Brussels, 13 July 2011, p. 19.

[65] GDPR, Recital 32.

[66] Article 29 Working Party, Guidelines on consent under Regulation 2016/679, WP259 rev.01, Brussels, 10.04.2018, p. 11.

*3. Clear separation of information related to obtaining consent for data pro-
cessing activities from information about other matters."*

As can be seen above, user control and transparency for the data subject are strongly
related with the "specific consent". Granularity, requires controller to provide separate
opt-in for each purpose.

3.2.1.4   Unambiguous Indication of wishes

Statement or clear affirmative action needs to be provided by the data subject so that the
consent is valid. Recital 32 states that consent can be collected through a written or (a
recorded) oral statement, including by electronic means. According to the WP29, pre-ticked
boxes or opt-out constructions that require an intervention from the data subject to prevent
agreement are not allowed by the GDPR.[67] On that matter, Advocate General in Planet24 case
states *"... it is not sufficient in this respect if the user's declaration of consent is pre-
formulated and if the user must actively object when he does not agree with the processing of
data. Indeed, in the latter situation, one does not know whether such a pre-formulated text has
been read and digested. The situation is not unambiguous. ... In such a situation, it is not
possible to establish whether consent has been freely given.".[68]*

3.2.2   Direct Marketing as Legitimate Interest of the Controller

Legitimate interest of the controller is one of the independent legal grounds regulated under
Art. 6(f) of the GDPR. Legitimate interest is carried out with a balancing test between the
interest of the controller, or any third parties to whom the data is disclosed, and the interests
and fundamental rights of the data subjects. According to the WP29, "legitimate interest"
must be lawful, specific enough to allow the balancing test and represent a real and present
interests.[69]

---

[67] Ibid, p.16.

[68] Planet49 GmbH v. Bundesverband der Verbraucherzentralen und Verbraucherverbände – Verbraucherzentrale
Bundesverband e.V. (C-673/17), Opinion of Advocate General, 21 March 2019, para. 61 and 62.

[69] Article 29 Working Party, Opinion 06/2014 on the "Notion of legitimate interests of the data controller under
Article 7 of Directive 95/46/EC, 09.04.2014, p. 25

In recital 47 of the GDPR, it is stated that personal data processing for direct marketing purposes may be regarded within the scope of legitimate interest.[70] However, as WP29 states in its opinion on the matter: *"this does not mean the controllers would be able to rely on Art. 7(f) to unduly monitor the on-line or off-line activities of their costumers, combine vast amounts of data about them from different sources that were initially collected in other contexts and for different purposes, and create - and, for example, with the intermediary of data brokers, also trade in - complex profiles of the customers' personalities and preferences without their knowledge, a workable mechanism to object, let alone informed consent. Such a profiling activity is likely to present a significant intrusion into the privacy of the customer, and when this is so, the controller's interest would be overridden by the interests and rights of the data subject."[71]*

With the developing technology for targeted behavioural advertisements such as profiling with automated methods, it is clear that the object of the balancing exercise has changed. Even though the issue was more about right to free commercial speech before, nowadays it became about the economic interests of businesses to track and monitor the profiles and the behaviours of the customers, as personal data is a great value as an asset. The economic interests of the businesses must be balanced against the fundamental rights to privacy and protection of personal data of the individuals.[72]

Accordingly, even though legitimate interest is a broad concept which includes direct marketing it does not necessarily mean that it could be used for any direct marketing purposes. The balance between economic interests of the businesses and fundamental rights of the data subjects must be maintained.

---

[70] GDPR, Recital 47.
[71] WP29, Opinion 06/2014, p. 26.
[72] Ibid, p. 46.

3.3   Data Subjects' Rights under GDPR and Enforcements

3.3.1   Right to be Informed

3.3.1.1   Controllers' Obligation to Inform the Data Subject

The right to be informed is strictly related to the transparency principle under GDPR. The controllers are obliged to provide information to the data subjects prior to the processing, regarding on which purposes and how the data are collected, which personal data are collected, used and processed. Moreover, the data subjects must be made aware of the risks, safeguards and their rights regarding processing.[73] Information to be provided to data subjects are listed under Art. 13 of the GDPR. If the personal data is obtained from other sources and not from the data subject directly, the controller must notify the data subject about the source of the personal data.[74] The right to lodge a complaint with a supervisory authority in case of a data breach must be provided to data subjects by the controller.[75] If the data subject already has the information mentioned above, the obligation to inform does not apply.[76]

In cases the processing includes automated-decision making, the controller should provide information first about the processing which involves automated-decision making and how the logic of the AI works and possible consequences of the processing.[77]

3.3.1.2   Right of Access by the Data Subject

Apart from the obligations of the controller to provide information, data subjects have the right to obtain information from the controller whether or not personal data concerning the data subject are being processed as well as other information listed under Art. 15 of the GDPR. Moreover, the controller is obliged to provide a copy of the personal data undergoing processing.[78]

---

[73] GDPR, Recital 39.
[74] GDPR, Art. 13 (2) and 14 (2).
[75] GDPR, Art. 13 (2) (d) and 14 (2) (e).
[76] GDPR, Art. 13 (4) and 14 (5) (a).
[77] GDPR, Art. 13 (2) and 14 (2) (f).
[78] GDPR, Art. 15 (5).

Even though the data subjects have the right to obtain information about the existence of automated decision-making and its logic as mentioned above, there is no obligation in the GDPR for the controller to provide information about outcomes of the processing, such as the profile made or is being made on the certain data subject. [79]

3.3.2   Right to Rectification and Right to be Forgotten

Since the accuracy of personal data is essential, right to rectification is regulated under Art. 16 of the GDPR. A rectification right for the data subject is also an obligation for the controller to correct the inaccurate personal data undue delay.[80] This right includes further a right to complete the personal data or adding supplementary statements.

The right to be forgotten, allows the data subjects to request the deletion of their own data from the controller.[81] The controller is obliged to erase the data undue delay when; the personal data is no longer necessary for the purposes it was collected, the data subject withdraws consent, the data subject objects to the processing and there are no overriding legitimate grounds, the data processed unlawfully, there is a need to erase the data to comply with another Member State and the data have been collected to offer information society services to children.[82] There are some exceptions to the right to be forgotten regulated under Art. 17(2) of the GDPR. Right to be forgotten includes also the personal data that has been backed up or archived. Although, the legislators regulated the right to be forgotten in general, no further clarification has been provided for the application of the right in a technical manner by the controllers. Accordingly, the companies could face major challenges for tempering with the long-term archival storage, especially regarding the automated decision-making processes.[83]

---

[79] GDPR, Art. 15 (1) (h).

[80] GDPR, Art. 16.

[81] GDPR, Art. 17.

[82] Ibid.

[83] Politou, Eugenia, Alexandra Michota, Efthimios Alepis, Matthias Pocs, and Constantinos Patsakis. "Backups and the Right to Be Forgotten in the GDPR: An Uneasy Relationship." Computer Law & Security Review: The International Journal of Technology Law and Practice 34, no. 6 (2018), p. 1256.

3.3.3 Right to Restriction of Processing

According to Art. 18 of the GDPR, data subjects have the right to restrict the controller temporarily from processing their personal data if the accuracy of the personal data is contested, if the processing is unlawful and data subject requests the personal data to be restricted instead of erased, if the data is required for exercise or defence of claims and if there is a pending decision on the legitimate interests of the controller override the interests of the data subject.[84] Restricting the processing of personal data methods can include temporarily moving the selected data to another processing system, making the selected personal data unavailable to users, or temporarily removing published data from a website.[85] The controller must notify the data subject before the restriction of processing is lifted.[86] A notification obligation for the controller to each recipient to whom personal data is disclosed, unless it is impossible or a disproportionate effort and to data subject upon request pertaining to those recipients is regulated under Art. 19 of the GDPR.

3.3.4 Right to Data Portability

The data portability right allows data subjects to receive the data concerning them from the controller in a "*structured, commonly used and machine-readable format*" or transmit the data from former controller to another controller in cases only when the processing is based on consent or the data is necessary for the performance of a contract and is carried out by automated means.[87] Data controllers are expected to transmit personal data in an interoperable format.[88] If it is possible to transmit the data by technical means, the data subject has the right to request the transmission directly from a controller to another controller.[89]

Although data portability as a right is quite limited, it has a potential for effective individual control over their data. How to implement the right technically is not certain and the format of the data provided is being chosen by the controller. However, overall the new right to data

---

[84] GDPR, Art. 18.
[85] GDPR, Recital 67.
[86] GDPR, Art. 18(3).
[87] GDPR, Art. 20.
[88] GDPR, Recital 68.
[89] GDPR, Art. 20(2).

portability gives the data subject more control over his/her data. There are some ways to make the right even more effective as provided by Ursic;[90]

"(i) establishing control over personal data transfers,

(ii) enabling (re)use of personal data,

(iii) enabling a better understanding of data flows, and

(iv) facilitating equality and allowing free development of personality."

Even though there were different interpretations for the implementation of this right, it can be said that WP29 interpreted the right in a broader way.[91] As the data, subject to the right to data portability, must be provided by the data subject to the controller, WP29 interprets "provided by" including *"the personal data that are observed from the activities of users such as raw data processed by a smart meter or other types of connected objects, activity logs, history of website usage or search activities."*[92] However this type of data does not include the data created by the controller based on the raw personal data collected.[93]

According to the WP29, "personal data concerning the data" subject could be interpreted broadly and therefore, data-set including third-party data can be transmitted to the new controller.[94] The third-party data received by the new controller cannot be used for its own purposes such as using the data to enrich the profile of the third-party data subject. Even though the new controller is responsible for finding a legal ground for the data including third-parties' personal data, it seems that this interpretation allows data portability without the knowledge of the other data subjects included in the data-set.[95] However, in practice it does not seem realistic that the data controllers would not use the data regarding third persons to enrich the existing profilin on them, especially the companies providing online advertising services.

---

[90] H. Ursic. "Unfolding the New-Born Right to Data Portability: Four Gateways to Data Subject Control." SCRIPTed: A Journal of Law, Technology & Society 15, no. 1 (2018), p.67.

[91] See De Hert, Papakonstantinou, Malgieri, Beslay, and Sanchez. "The Right to Data Portability in the GDPR: Towards User-centric Interoperability of Digital Services." Computer Law & Security Review: The International Journal of Technology Law and Practice 34, no. 2 (2018), p. 203.

[92] Ibid., p. 9-10.

[93] Ibid.

[94] Ibid., p. 11-12.

[95] Reins, Leonie. "Regulating New Technologies in Uncertain Times". Vol. 32. Information Technology and Law Series. The Hague (2019), p. 143.

3.3.5   Right to Object

Data subjects have a right to object to the data processing on the grounds that relate to their particular situation or when the data is processed for direct marketing purposes.[96] The right can be exercised by automated means using technical specifications.

The right to object aims to balance between the data subjects' data protection rights and the legitimate interests of the controller when it is used on the bases of data subjects' particular situation. The CJEU ruled that in general the data subjects' rights override the economic interest of the controller on the criteria of *"the nature of the information in question and its sensitivity for the data subject's private life and on the interest of the public in having that information."*[97] The burden of proof for proving that the legal grounds for data processing are legitimate is on the controller. After the data subject invokes the right effectively, the data controller cannot process the data referred to in the objection. However, the data processing took place regarding the data subjects' data before the objection remains legitimate.

The personal data in question must be unconditionally erased or anonymised regarding the objections to processing for direct marketing purposes.[98] The controllers providing information society services are also obliged to provide the procedures and technical tools for exercising the right.

If the personal data is processed for scientific or historical research purposes or statistical purposes, the data subject, on grounds relating to his or her particular situation, has the right to object to processing of personal data concerning him or her, with the exception of the processing is necessary for the performance of a task carried out for reasons of public interest.[99]

---

[96] GDPR, Art. 21.

[97] Google Spain SL, Google Inc. v. Agencia Española de Protección de Datos (AEPD), Mario Costeja González, C-131/12, (CJEU, 13.05.2014), para. 81.

[98] Council of Europe," Explanatory Report to the Protocol amending the Convention for the Protection of Individuals with regard to Automatic Processing of Personal Data", No.223, (10.10.2018), p.79.

[99] GDPR, Art. 21(6).

3.4   Enforcements under GDPR

Data subjects' have the right to lodge a complaint to a supervisory authority in cases of violation of their rights or unlawful processing of their data, along with their right to an effective judicial remedy and, to receive compensation against the supervisory authority and controller or processor.[100] Data subjects also have the right to be represented by a non-profit organisation.[101]

GDPR authorizes the supervisory authorities of the Member States to impose administrative fines for infringements of the regulation.[102] GDPR regulates a two-tier approach for fines. The supervisory authorities can impose administrative fines up to 10 000 000 EUR, or in the case of an undertaking, up to 2 % of the total worldwide annual turnover of the preceding financial year, whichever is higher.[103] For the infringements such as; breaches of the basic principles for processing and the conditions for consent, breaches of data subjects' rights and of the regulation's provisions governing the transfer of personal data to recipients in third countries, the supervisory authorities impose the fines up to € 20,000,000 or, in the case of an undertaking, 4 % of its total worldwide annual turnover.[104] For the determination of the fine amount in each case some criteria must be taken into account, such as nature, gravity and duration of the infringement taking into account the nature scope or purpose of the processing concerned as well as the number of data subjects affected and the level of damage suffered by them.[105]

3.5   Concluding Remarks

GDPR, sets a particular focus on ensuring and protecting the fundamental rights of the data subjects. In that regard, it is particularly important that the principle of fair and lawful processing could be interpreted in a way to protect the data subjects against the controllers in a monopoly position in the market. Since, consent is most commonly used legal basis for data processing, the monopoly position of the companies affects the validity of the consent for data processing. According to the Report of the Special Barometer 487a, only %22 of the respond-

---

[100] GDPR, Art. 77, 78 and 79.
[101] GDPR, Art. 80.
[102] GDPR, Art. 83(1).
[103] GDPR, Art. 83(4).
[104] GDPR, Art. 83(5).
[105] GDPR, Art. 83(2).

ents say that they are always informed about the coons regarding the collections and use of their personal data online.[106] The results also indicate that the amount of the respondents reading privacy statements fully are limited to %13.[107] And the main reason for not reading the statements fully indicated as the respondents find them too long(%66) or difficult to understand (%31).[108] As the results of the reports also demonstrate, data processing solely based on the consent of the users, could be insufficient to protect the data subjects from abusive data processing activities. Especially, in the cases of existing clear imbalance between the controllers and data subjects.

Even though GDPR is a great improvement regarding the rights of the data subjects, some weak points in the Regulation still exists for the protection the fundamental rights of the data subjects. Existing technical problems make it difficult for the controllers to fully comply with the GDPR, such as black-box problem for providing the logic behind decision of the automated decision-making systems of the AIs or fully erasure of the data also from the back-ups or archives, without effecting the decision-making process. Also, the technical uncertainty regarding the exercising of the data portability right and retention periods remains.

Also, an obligation for the controller is to provide information about the outcomes of the processing based on the profiling and automated decision-making systems, does not exist. Even though, it is problematic regarding the trade secrets and competition law, the Cambridge Analytica scandal has shown on what degree the right to privacy could be violated when the personal data are combined.

Regarding the effectiveness of the enforcements in the GDPR, it is clear that the increased amount of the fines makes many the small- and medium-sized enterprises more motivated to comply with the GDPR. Even though, international big companies are not affected as much financially, these companies are motivated to comply with the GDPR in order to keep their good reputation in the eyes of the customers. [109]

---

[106] European Comission, "Special Eurobarometer 487a Report", GDPR, (2019), p. 42.

[107] Ibid., p.47.

[108] Ibid., p. 51.

[109] Ceross, Aaron. "Examining Data Protection Enforcement Actions through Qualitative Interviews and Data Exploration." International Review of Law, Computers & Technology 32, no. 1 (2018): p. 107.

4 Profiling and Automated Individual Decision Making under GDPR

With the development of artificial intelligence (AI) and machine learning technology, automated decision-making and profiling are used in many sectors, especially for direct marketing purposes.

Profiling defined as *"any form of automated processing of personal data consisting of the use of personal data to evaluate certain personal aspects relating to a natural person, in particular to analyse or predict aspects concerning that natural person's performance at work, economic situation, health, personal preferences, interests, reliability, behaviour, location or movements"* in Art. 4(4) of the GDPR. Some scholars criticize the definition of profiling in the GDPR on the grounds that profiling consists of different stages and therefore each stage might include some or all characteristics mentioned above.[110]

Automated decisions are decisions made by technical means, without any human involvement. Often automated decisions are based on the profiling of data subject,[111] but not necessarily, since the scope of the profiling and automated decision making could differ.[112]

General principles of the GDPR mentioned above; such as transparency, lawfulness, fairness, purpose limitation, data minimisation etc. apply when the personal data processing is within the definition of Art. 22(1) of the GDPR. The conditions for automated decision-making are regulated under Article 22 of the GDPR. According to the definition in Art.22(1) for data processing to be considered automated individual decision-making:

1- A decision must be made
2- The decision must be based solely on automated processing

---

[110] Rustici, Chiara. "GDPR Profiling and Business Practice." Computer Law Review International 19, no. 2 (2018), p. 34.

[111] Steppe, Richard. "Online Price Discrimination and Personal Data: A General Data Protection Regulation Perspective." Computer Law & Security Review: The International Journal of Technology Law and Practice 33, no. 6 (2017), p. 783.

[112] Art. 29 Data Protection Working Party, Guidelines on Automated individual decision-making and Profiling for the purposes of Regulation 2016/679, (2018), p. 8 and Kamlah, W.. In K. U. Plath (Ed.), „BDSG/DSGVO Kommentar zum BDSG und zur DSGVO sowie den Datenschutzbestimmungen von TMG und TKG" (2nd ed.). Cologne: Otto Schmidt, (2016), Art. 22 margin note 2.

3- The decision must produce legal effects concerning the data subjects or affect the data subjects significantly.

Regarding the obligations of controllers, the controllers are obliged to implement suitable measures to safeguard the data subjects' rights and freedoms and legitimate interests, at least the right to obtain human intervention on the part of the controller. [113] Accordingly, the data subjects may express their point of view and contest the decision. Moreover, the right to obtain an explanation of the decision reached after such assessment is regulated under recital 71 of the GDPR. The controller is also obliged to *"provide information about the existence of automated decision-making, including profiling, referred to in Art. 22 (1) and (4) GDPR and, at least in those cases, give meaningful information about the logic involved, as well as the significance and the envisaged consequences of such processing for the data subject."[114]* According to Art. 15 of the GDPR, the data subject has the right to obtain from the controller confirmation as to whether or not personal data concerning him or her are being processed. Data subjects should be informed in case of an existence of automated decision-making, including profiling with meaningful information about the logic involved, as well as the significance and the envisaged consequences of such processing for the data subject. Finally, the controller needs to explain simply the rationale behind the decision or the criteria playing an essential role for the decision to be taken by the AI, so that the data subject can challenge the decision if necessary. [115]

Even though the rights of individuals are protected under the GDPR regarding making individual decisions verifiable and rectifiable, user rights and the principle of transparency do not provide protection for discrimination issues of the AIs. [116]

---

[113] GDPR, Art. 22(2).

[114] GDPR, Art. 13-14.

[115] WP29, Guidelines for Automated Individual Decision Making and Profiling, (2018), p. 25.

[116] Dreyer,S., Schulz W. , "The General Data Protection Regulation and Automated Decision-making: Will it deliver?", BertelsmannStiftung (2019), https://www.bertelsmann-stiftung.de/fileadmin/files/BSt/Publikationen/GrauePublikationen/GDPR.pdf (Accessed: 28.09.2019), p. 45. For for more information on discrimination see: World Economic Forum "How to Prevent Discriminatory Outcomes in Machine Learning", (2018) http://www3.weforum.org/docs/WEF_40065_White_Paper_How_to_Prevent_Discriminatory_Outcomes_in_Machine_Learning.pdf (Accessed: 20.09.2019).

4.1 The Right not to be Subject to Automated Decision based on Profiling

The right not to be subject to a decision solely based on automated processing is regulated under Art. 22(1) of the GDPR. This right can be exercised only when there is a legal effect concerning the data subject or significantly affects him or her, such as the *"automatic refusal of an online credit application or e-recruiting practices without any human intervention"*.[117] This right could be interpreted as a prohibition regardless of its exercise by the data subject.[118]

Art. 22(2) of the GDPR regulates some exceptions: automated decision-making or profiling is necessary to enter, performance or concluding a contract between data subject and the controller or data subject giving his/her explicit consent for or Member State law, which the controller is subject to and which also lays down suitable measures to safeguard the data subject's rights and freedoms and legitimate interests. The controller thus needs to *"implement suitable measures to safeguard the data subject's rights and freedoms and legitimate interests, at least the right to obtain human intervention on the part of the controller, to express his or her point of view and to contest the decision"* in the first two cases.[119]

4.2 Online Behavioural Advertising

Online behavioural advertising can be defined as *"the practice of monitoring people's online behaviour and using the collected information to show people individually targeted advertisements."*[120] Advertisements are one of the main sources of revenue in the tech industry. These data are vital for the tech companies since it helps the companies to develop new products and services or to improve the current services and products to create better advertisements so as to attract more customers. Especially for companies like Facebook and Google, as their services for the users are free of charge in exchange for the data of the users

---

[117] GDPR, Recital 71.

[118] WP29, "Guidelines on Automated individual decision-making and Profiling for the purposes of Regulation 2016/679", WP251rev.01, 06.02.2018 and Martini, M. In B. Paal & D. A. Pauly (Eds.), „Datenschutz-Grundverordnung Bundesdatenschutzgesetz (2nd ed.)". Munich: C.H. Beck. (2018).

[119] GDPR, Art. 22(3)

[120] Boerman, Sophie C, Sanne Kruikemeier, and Frederik J Zuiderveen Borgesius. "Online Behavioral Advertising: A Literature Review and Research Agenda." Journal of Advertising 46, no. 3 (2017), p. 364.

to be used mostly in profiling[121] and behavioural advertising activities. The importance of the situation regarding privacy cannot be ignored, considering the number of individual profiles of Facebook and Google, 2.7 billion people and Google's are not less than Facebook's.[122]

The advertisement systems of Google and Facebook are based on real-time bidding. Real-time bidding is *"An auction for the buying and selling of display advertising inventory by individual impressions in a bidding system that operates in real time."[123]* A research conducted on a worldwide level indicates that Facebook uses sensitive data for advertising purposes and %67 of the users are tagged with potentially sensitive ad preference.[124] Furthermore, the scholars demonstrated the fact that the GDPR had no significant impact on Facebook to prevent the usage of potentially sensitive ad preferences for advertising purposes.[125] Also, there are allegations on Google that the company enables data transfers with "hidden push pages" taking place in the real-time bidding systems without valid consent of the users.[126]

4.3   Cookies

Cookies are small computer files, which contain the data stored in the web browsers and related to HTTP request.[127] As mentioned above, in order for Google and Facebook to provide a useful target marketing, cookies must be involved along with the other techniques of tracking.[128] The tracking can be done directly (first-party cookies) or indirectly (third-party cookies) connected to cookies in order to keep the records of the visited websites and create profiles based on them.

---

[121] For more technical information on profiling see: Hildebrandt, Mireille, and Serge Gutwirth. Profiling the European Citizen: Cross-disiplinary Perspectives. S.l.: Springer, 2008.

[122] Facebook , "Company Info," (2019), http://newsroom.fb.com/company-info/ (Accessed:10.08.2019)

[123] Doyle, Charles. "Real-time Bidding." A Dictionary of Marketing, 2016, A Dictionary of Marketing.

[124] Cuevas, Ángel, Cabañas, José González, Arrate, Aritz, and Cuevas, Rubén. "Does Facebook Use Sensitive Data for Advertising Purposes? Worldwide Analysis and GDPR Impact." 2019, p.3.

[125] Ibid., p. 5.

[126] See Chapter 6.2.1.1 for more information about the topic.

[127] Kristol, David. "HTTP Cookies: Standards, Privacy, and Politics." ACM Transactions on Internet Technology (TOIT) 1, no. 2 (2001): 157.

[128] Tene, Omer, and Polonetsky, Jules. "To Track or "do Not Track": Advancing Transparency and Individual Control in Online Behavioral Advertising." Minnesota Journal of Law, Science & Technology 13, no. 1 (2012), p. 245 and 249.

Even though cookies are generally regulated under the GDPR, E-privacy Directive particularises and complements the GDPR, mainly by regulating the usage of the cookies.[129] It can be said that EPD is *lex specialis* to the GDPR.[130] The Directive stated in Art. 5(3) that activities such as *"the storing information, or the gaining of access to information already stored, in the terminal equipment"* including cookies but not limited to.[131] Since 2009, (prior) informed consent is necessary for the storage of the cookies.

Very recently, further clarifications are provided regarding consent for the cookies in the decision of the case *Planet49* by the ECJ.[132] Advocate General states in his opinion that preticket cookie checkbox was no active consent and therefore invalid, as well as bundled consent instead of separated.[133] Furthermore, the consent must not only indicate unambiguously data subjects' wishes but also a clear affirmative action needs to be taken by the data subject to signify the agreement to the processing of personal data.[134] The court followed the opinion of the Advocate General in its' decision.[135] Furthermore, the Court ruled that the information the service provider is responsible of giving the users includes *"... the duration of the operation of cookies and whether or not third parties may have access to those cookies."*[136]

According to recital 25, cookies should be intended for a legitimate purpose such as analysing the effectiveness of website advertising. The users should be informed clearly and precisely about the purposes of cookies and similar devices, and the opportunity to refuse must be offered. Where the information collected includes personal data in the scope of the GDPR,

---

[129] Directive 2002/58/EC of the European Parliament and of the Council of 12 July 2002 concerning the processing of personal data and the protection of privacy in the electronic communications sector (Directive on privacy and electronic communications) as amended by Directive 2006/24/EC and Directive 2009/136/EC.

[130] GDPR, Art. 95.

[131] It also refers to spyware, webbugs or hidden identifiers etc. (EDP, Recital 24)

[132] Planet49 GmbH v. Bundesverband der Verbraucherzentralen und Verbraucherverbände – Verbraucherzentrale Bundesverband e.V., C-673/17, (CJEU, 01.10.2019).

[133] Planet49 GmbH v. Bundesverband der Verbraucherzentralen und Verbraucherverbände – Verbraucherzentrale Bundesverband e.V. (C-673/17), Opinion of Advocate General, 21 March 2019, para. 61-62.

[134] Planet49, C-673/17, Opinion, para. 70.

[135] Planet49, C-673/17, Decision, para. 59.

[136] Planet49, C-673/17, Decision, para. 81.

GDPR will also apply.[137] The CJEU case-law also confirms that when processing falls within the material scope of the EPD and the GDPR, both might apply at the same time.[138]

The mechanisms of the GDPR do not apply to the enforcement of the national implementation of the EPD.[139] Since the EDP causes different legislations across Europe, the Commission aims to increase the level of harmonisation via E-privacy Regulation, although the EPR is currently still in progress.[140]

4.3.1   Cookie Policies

Since Google and Facebook are two dominating companies, along with their parent companies and subsidiaries, it is necessary to analyse their privacy policies for cookies within the scope of this book. For the assessment; an indication of values, purposes, third-party companies, retention in the policy are taken into consideration.

It seems that generally these companies or their subsidiaries fail to comply with the GDPR and EPD regarding transparency, purpose specification and retention. For instance, even though Facebook and Google provide sufficient information, that information is provided through links, which are connected to further links. This situation might result in the users' not reaching to comprehensive information about third parties, on what purposes the data is used etc., which in some policies are not mentioned or mentioned in very generic terms. It must be also kept in mind that, the data collected through these companies' third-party tracking activities in other websites via cookies are countless and hard to keep the record with. This can cause high risks of privacy, as well as disclosure of sensitive data without users' consent as proven by Maris, Libert and Henrichsen that Google (Alphabet and its

---

[137] Data Protection Working Party, Opinion 2/2010 on online behavioural advertising, 22 June 2010, WP, p. 29.

[138] Wirtschaftsakademie, C-210/16 (CJEU, 5 June 2018), para. 33-34.

[139] EDPB, Opinion 5/2019 on the interplay between the ePrivacy Directive and the GDPR, in particular regarding the competence, tasks and powers of data protection authorities, 12 March 2019, p. 25.

[140] Proposal for a Regulation of the European Parliament and of the Council concerning the respect for private life and the protection of personal data in electronic communications and repealing Directive 2002/58/EC (Regulation on Privacy and Electronic Communications), Brussels, 10.1.2017, 2017/0003(COD).

subsidiaries, including Google Analytics) tracks %74 of porn sites with third-party cookies to use the data for profiling and sophisticated behavioural advertising purposes.[141]

The cookie policies include information only about how "direct tracking" is taking place and solely the information, that third-party companies have access to the data collected by Google and Facebook. However, a complete list of third-parties is not mentioned in the privacy policies of both companies.

4.3.1.1 Google and Youtube

Google.com is among the top five tracking domains along with Doubleclick, which is also owned by Alphabet Inc.[142] Since Google is dominating the market, it is essential that the company provides enough information on how the tracking is taking place, for which purposes and how the data is used.[143]

The cookie policy of Google is a bit vague one and it can be seen that they have adopted a simple and general one.[144] Google provides general information about cookies, including links to "ad settings", "types of cookies used by Google", "advertising cookies" and "privacy policy". The ad personalization can be turned off for Google and its partners. However, it does not limit the advertising, nor the collection of data, since it can be based on users' general location, IP address, browser type and search terms.

Even though there is a list of cookie types provided, it is not very comprehensive. The settings for cookies are only possible for the advertisement cookies, not with other types of cookies. Google provided a list of domains they use to set cookies for advertising products. However, there is no information about third-party cookies collected by Google at all. In general, information about retention policy lacks in the policy of Google, but Google Analytics' and

---

[141] Maris, Elena, Timothy Libert, and Jennifer Henrichsen. "Tracking Sex: The Implications of Widespread Sexual Data Leakage and Tracking on Porn Websites." 2019, p. 5.

[142] Gribing Arlfors, Christian, and Simon Nilsson. "Tracking the Cookies: A Quantitative Study on User Perceptions about Online Tracking." 2019, p. 20.

[143] Statcounter Netmarketshare. Search Engine Market Share United States of America, 2019. Available at: http://gs.statcounter.com (Accessed: 04.09.2019)

[144] Google, 2019, "Cookie Policy". Available at: https://policies.google.com/technologies/cookies?hl=en-US (Accessed: 03.09.2019)

Alphabet.Inc's policies are quite comprehensive, including technical information regarding cookies, purposes, values and retention.[145] Finally, it could be said that the cookie policy of Google can be optimised.

Recently, Google Chrome took an action against third party cookies by blocking them.[146] Even though it is on behalf of user privacy and for increasing transparency, it does strengthen the hand of Google by reducing the competition.

Within the light of these facts, it is undeniable that Google has a dominant position in the market and as the research shows above, the company collects personal data, including sensitive data without valid consent of the data subjects. The state of art regarding privacy of the individuals does not seem bright, within the light of the previous privacy incidents by Google and the privacy incidents waiting to be proven.

4.3.1.2   Facebook, Instagram, WhatsApp

On the contrary to Google, Facebook's cookie policy is quite comprehensive.[147] The information of values, purposes, retention policy, what data they collect through cookies, where they use the cookies and especially, a list including some of the third-party companies which use cookies on the Facebook Services are provided. Proper links are provided to Facebook Ads and Ad Settings, if the user has a Facebook account. Moreover, Facebook provided links for opting out of seeing online interest-based ads; such as Digital Advertising Alliance (United States), Digital Advertising Alliance of Canada and European Interactive Digital Advertising Alliance. Opposite to Google, users can see and control easily on which criteria they see the ads.

---

[145] Google Analytics Cookie Usage on Websites. Available at: https://developers.google.com/analytics/devguides/collection/analyticsjs/cookie-usage (Accessed: 04.09.2019) and Alphabet Cookie Policy. Available at: https://www.alphabet.com/en-ww/cookies (Accessed: 04.09.2019)

[146] Chromium Blog, Improving Privacy and Security on the Web, 07.05.2019. Available at: https://blog.chromium.org/2019/05/improving-privacy-and-security-on-web.html (Accessed: 04.09.2019)

[147] Facebook, Cookies & Other Storage Technologies. Available at: https://www.facebook.com/policy/cookies/ (Accessed: 04.09.2019)

WhatsApp, a subsidiary of Facebook, on the other hand does not include any specific information by any means.[148] The cookie policy is bundled up with terms of service, privacy policy etc. in a long document called "WhatsApp Legal Info". Not only is the information too generic and does not include any specific information regarding the purposes, values, retention, but also there is no link to adjust the cookie settings. WhatsApp allows the settings only through users' browser or device with the warning that disabling cookies might cause function errors. On the contrary, Facebook provides a list of third-party and advertising cookies along with settings for the ad-cookies, WhatsApp does not even mention the third-party cookies.

When it comes to Instagram, the policy is a bit more detailed than WhatsApp but not even close to Facebook.[149] The policy includes very generic information general on cookies but not about the cookie types Instagram uses. The policy contains wide and vague purposes for the usage of cookies, which are far away from being specific and transparent to users. Even though they include information on the duration of storage for the cookies, they did not include any list for third-party cookies. Retention is not mentioned in the policy. The links for institutions for managing cookies mentioned above are provided.

Apart from the analysis of the cookie privacy policy of Facebook and it's subsidiaries in theory, the reality of the data collecting through cookies tells another story regarding privacy.[150] As is known, in order to use Facebook' social network, the individuals have to accept that Facebook may collect many data outside of the Facebook website in the internet or on smartphone apps and assign these data to the respective Facebook user account. The third-party sources for data include not only the usage by other services of Facebook like WhatsApp and Instagram, but also use of third-party websites and apps, through "Facebook Business Tools". Accordingly, these data can be combined by Facebook, even if users have blocked web tracking in their browser or device settings. Finally, separate consent for each of these tracking activities are not collected by the Facebook.

---

[148] " Whatsapp Legal Info" (2019). Available at: https://www.whatsapp.com/legal/ (Accessed: 04.09.2019)

[149] "Instagram, About Cookies". Available at: https://help.instagram.com/1896641480634370?ref=ig (Accessed: 04.09.2019)

[150] See Chapter 6.2.2.2. for more information.

5   International Transfers and Flows of Personal Data

First of all, it is necessary to determine what constitutes the territorial scope of the GDPR before one goes through the cross-border data transfers. In this section the data flows between U.S and the EU is particularly important since both Facebook and Google are U.S based tech companies. Therefore, after clarifying the territorial scope of the GDPR, the regulations for data transfers between U.S and EU will be analysed regarding the relevant progressions in the field.

5.1   Territorial Scope of the GDPR

Territorial scope of the GDPR for processing personal data by the controller and processor is determined on the criteria that whether they have an establishment in the EU, if they have targeting and monitoring activities in the EU or where public international law applies when the controller is not established in the Union.[151] The establishments of the controllers and processors must be considered separately.[152] The term "establishment" is interpreted broadly by the CJEU, when determining whether an entity based outside the EU has an establishment in a Member State. CJEU ruled that the concept of establishment extends *"to any real and effective activity — even a minimal one — exercised through stable arrangements".[153]* The Court ruled in the Google Spain case that the concept of "processing in the activities of an establishment" is also broad by stating that *"the activities of the operator of the search engine and those of its establishment situated in the Member State concerned are inextricably linked since the activities relating to the advertising space constitute the means of rendering the search engine at issue economically profitable and that engine is, at the same time, the means enabling those activities to be performed."[154]* Accordingly, only the location of data processing is irrelevant to determine the territorial scope of the GDPR. Moreover, the rules on territorial scope are not derogable.[155] EDPB recommends a two-level approach for applications of the targeting criterion, first determining whether the processing relates to personal

---

[151] GDPR, Art.3.

[152] EDPB, "Guidelines 3/2018 on the territorial scope of the GDPR (Article 3)- Version for public consultation," 16.10.2018 ,p. 9.

[153] Weltimmo s. r. o. v. Nemzeti Adatvédelmi és Információszabadság Hatóság, C-230/14, (CJEU, 1.10.2015), para. 31.

[154] Google Spain, C-131/12, para. 56.

[155] EDPB, "Guidelines 3/2018 on the territorial scope of the GDPR (Article 3)", p. 4.

data of data subjects who are in the Union, and secondly if it relates to the offering of goods or services or to the monitoring of data subjects' behaviour in the Union.[156]

5.2   Cross-Border Data Flows Between U.S and the EU

The GDPR regulates that *"any transfer of personal data which are undergoing processing or are intended for processing after transfer to a third country or to an international organisation"* are allowed only when they comply with the Chapter V of the GDPR.[157] Accordingly, personal data transfers can take place only when there is an adequacy decision provided by the European Commission or where the controller or processor provides appropriate safeguards.[158]

Regarding the data transfers for commercial purposes to the US, European Commission adopted an adequacy decision in 2000 so-called "Safe Harbour principles.[159] However, the CJEU declared Safe Harbour invalid in Schrems case and a new decision for adequacy was adopted in 2016 called EU-US Privacy Shield.[160] The judgment regarding Schrems was a landmark decision, by defining an adequate level of data protection and how the data protection rights in the EU can apply in third countries.[161] The EU-US Privacy Shield Framework allows the American companies to voluntarily to certificate themselves for data transfers from the EU.[162] The report of the Commission on the second annual review states that Privacy Shield still provides an adequate level of protection regarding the commercial matters.[163] However, the report adopted by the EDPB on the Second Annual Review of the EU-US

---

[156] EDPB, Guidelines 3/2018 on the territorial scope of the GDPR (Article 3), p. 13.

[157] GDPR, Art. 44.

[158] GDPR, Art. 45 and 46.

[159] Commission Decision 2000/520/EC of 26 July 2000 pursuant to Directive 95/46/EC of the European Parliament and of the Council on the adequacy of the protection provided by the safe harbour privacy principles and related frequently asked questions issued by the US Department of Commerce, OJ L 215.

[160] CJEU, Schrems , C-362/14 and Commission Implementing Decision (EU) 2016/1250 of 12 July 2016. pursuant to Directive 95/46/EC of the European Parliament and of the Council on the adequacy of the protection provided by the EU-U.S. Privacy Shield

[161] See Chapter 6.2.2.3 for more information on Case Schrems.

[162] Privacy Shield Framework, https://www.privacyshield.gov/welcome (Accessed: 29.09.2019)

[163] European Commission, Report From The Commission To The European Parliament And The Council on the second annual review of the functioning of the EU-U.S. Privacy Shield, Brussels, 19.12.2018.

Privacy Shield sets forth some criticism.[164] According to the EDPB, Privacy Shield does not provide protection against the indiscriminate collection and access of personal data for national security purposes.[165] The report indicates in general that the issues which resulted the invalidation of Safe Harbour currently remains. Moreover, some cases are still pending before the CJEU claiming that the E.U- U.S Privacy Shield does not provide adequate level of protection such as *La Quadrature du Net and Others v Commission* or *Schrems* cases.[166] Accordingly, there is a possibility that the EU-US Privacy Shield can be invalidated too.[167]

---

[164] EDPB, "EU - U.S. Privacy Shield - Second Annual Joint Review", 22. 01.2019

[165] Ibid., p. 6.

[166] La Quadrature du Net and Others v Commission, T-738/16,(CJEU, Action brought on 25 October 2016) and Data Protection Commissioner v Facebook Ireland Limited, Maximillian Schrems, C-311/18, (CJEU, Reference for a preliminary ruling from the High Court (Ireland) made on 9 May 2018).

[167] For more information see Chapter 6.2.2.3.

6 Compliance with the GDPR: Facebook and Google

Both the companies' incomes are mostly depending on targeted advertisements.[168] It is crucial for the purposes of this book to assess the privacy policy of the companies and to determine if they comply with the GDPR and if the GDPR is protective enough for the protection of the rights of the data subjects. Even though their privacy policies are relatively compliant with the GDPR, it does not necessarily mean that the activities of these companies are compliant with the GDPR, as will be seen in the following chapters.

6.1 Assessment of the Current Privacy Policies

Google and Facebook have updated their privacy policy quite often throughout time not only to comply with the GDPR, but also because of the evolving public pressure regarding privacy. In spite of the fact that the updated privacy policies by Google and Facebook are quite comprehensive, there are still some criterias mentioned in the GDPR that are not addressed, or even if addressed, addressed in a generic and vague manner. In the next chapters the privacy policies of Google and Facebook will be assessed based on the information provided in the privacy policies to the users along with the information provided regarding the data subjects' rights and whether necessary tools are provided to exercise them.

6.1.1 Facebook

The privacy policy of Facebook (last revised April 19, 2018) is written in a relatively plain language and easy to understand for an average data subject. Regarding the transparency, Facebook provides information about what kinds of data is collected, how the data is used, how and with whom is it shared, legal basis of the processing, how to exercise the rights provided under the GDPR, data retention, international data transfers and contact data of the Facebook with the contact of the related DPO. Apart from the information provided, Facebook Settings are available for privacy preferences.

---

[168] See Chapter 2 for more information on business activities of Facebook and Google.

6.1.1.1 Sources of Data, Purposes of Processing and Share of the Data

There are three sources for collecting personal data; the data provided by the users by using Facebook products, device information and information from Facebook's partners.[169] A very wide range of personal data are collected under the business activities of Facebook to be used for its business activities. This data is also combined with the data from other services of Facebook such as Instagram and WhatsApp. Accordingly, a numerous amount of data is collected by Facebook including sensitive data of the users.[170]

Even though the privacy settings allow the users to specify who sees their social media activity and how other people contact with the user, when it comes to data collection from various sources of Facebook there are no effective settings. Facebook allows the users only to specify settings for the location and face recognition data. Location data must be set off in each device used to access Facebook and the history can be deleted. As stated in the Terms of Service, users have to accept it simply by using Facebook. That enormous amount of data is then collected and processed by Facebook, either online or offline. In other words, regardless of the developments in the area of privacy, "take-it-or-leave-it" approach remains.

The purposes of the data processing indicated in the data policy as; providing, personalizing and improving Facebook products; providing measurement, analytics and other business services; promoting safety, integrity and security; communicating with the user and research-ing and innovating for social good. Although some simple explanations are provided in the privacy policy, the usage of data is stated in an extremely generic and abstract way. Moreo-ver, the information provided for the purposes are far from being sufficiently specific.[171] Therefore, the information provided by Facebook for data processing purposes generally do not meet the criteria of being specific.

The data provided directly by the users are shared with the people and accounts that are shared with depending on the settings. Also, all of this is the data are shared with the apps, websites and, third-party integrations on or using Facebook products along with the partners

---

[169] "Facebook Data Policy", https://www.facebook.com/policy.php (Accessed: 19.09.2019)
[170] For more information see Chapter 4.3.1.2.
[171] GDPR, Art. 6(1)(b) and Article 29 Working Party, "Opinion 03/2013 on Purpose Limitation", Brussels, 02.04.2013, p. 15.

using Facebook's analytics services, advertisers, partners offering goods and services in Facebook, vendors and service providers... In the Terms of Service, Facebook emphasizes that Facebook does not require any payment from the users for its services and that they do not sell personal data of the users to advertisers.[172] They claim that they do not share information with the advertisers that directly identifies the users. However, it does not mean that these data are anonymous and thus, outside the scope of the GDPR. Since the current technology allows de-anonymisation of the data to identify data subjects.

6.1.1.2   Legal Basis for Processing

Facebook collects personal data mainly on the grounds of consent, performance of a contract and legitimate interest.

Facebook can rely on the ground of "necessity for the performance of a contract" for processing necessary to provide services such as initial creation of a profile. With the initiation of the profile, the users allow Facebook to use the personal data and the content provided as well as intellectual property rights of the content according to the Terms of Service. However, this ground for data processing needs to be interpreted narrowly. Especially, when the business model of the company is considered, an interpretation allows unlimited data to be processed solely on the grounds of fulfilling the contract, which is not compatible with the purposes of the GDPR.

Facebook can also rely on the ground of "legitimate interest", but this legal basis of processing can only be used in the cases, where the individuals' interest or fundamental rights and freedoms are not outweighed. According to the privacy policy of Facebook, legitimate interest includes; providing accurate and reliable reporting to the advertisers and developers as well as improving advertiser businesses by evaluating the effectiveness of their online content when providing measurement, analytics and other business services. Direct marketing, research for academic reasons and sharing information with third parties including law enforcement to respond legal requests in order to prevent frauds and illegal activity are also listed as "legitimate interest".[173] However, there is no clear indication that legitimate data

---

[172] "Facebook Terms of Service", https://www.facebook.com/legal/terms/update (Accessed: 20.09.2019)

[173] https://www.facebook.com/about/privacy/legal_bases (Accessed: 20.09.2019)

processing can solely be based on ground of legitimate interest when the dominant position of Facebook is combined with the imposed far-reaching data processing conditions which data subjects do not have additional control mechanisms.[174]

Even though compliance with a legal obligation, protection of vital interests and public interest are mentioned as legal basis for data processing, as consent is main ground for the activities of Facebook; freely given, specific, informed and unambiguous consent must be provided by the users for the collection of certain types of data. The users have to accept that they agree with the Terms, Data Policy and Cookie Policy of Facebook when signing up actively by clicking the "sign up" button. An issue that needs to be addressed is whether the consent is freely given. It cannot be said that an effective consent is given by the data subject in the case of Facebook pursuant to dominant position of Facebook in the market. The users only accept the terms and policies to conclude the contract, which cannot be assessed as freely given consent under the GDPR. Moreover, regarding the unambiguous consent; "opt-out" mechanism Facebook offers from receiving targeted advertising does not necessarily deliver data subjects' consent.[175]

6.1.1.3 Data Subjects' Rights

Facebook informs the data subjects about right to access, rectify, port, object and erasure regulated under the GDPR. Moreover, offers a link to exercise these rights through Facebook Settings.[176]

6.1.1.3.1 Right to be Informed

Facebook provides generic information about data processing in its Data Policy and at the bottom of the Data Policy contact address of the data controller provided as Facebook Ireland Ltd. along with the contact information of the DPO. Regarding the data subjects' right to access, Facebook provides a service in the settings. The tool allows the users to see their

---

[174] Facebook, "Exploitative business terms pursuant to Section 19(1) GWB for inadequate data processing", Bundeskartelamt (B6-22/16) , 06.02.2019.

[175] Data Protection Working Party, "Opinion 2/2010 on online behavioural advertising, 22 June 2010", WP, p. 15.

[176] Facebook Settings, https://www.facebook.com/settings (Accessed: 23.09.2019)

categorised data or download all at once. Also, a link is provided in the Help section for further information requests regarding privacy.[177]

The categories under "Your information" consist of the data entered, uploaded and shared by the users and cover mainly the information which is already accessible to users when browsing their profile; such as messages, likes, comments and friends. The category "Information About You" includes the information associated with the users' accounts, such as ads, log in information, devices used and location. However, the data accessible by the users do not include the data associated with their accounts and collected through other websites or apps using Facebook services such as social plugins. Furthermore, no data is provided regarding the logic of the profiling and automated decision-making. The complete list of with whom personal data is shared is also not provided.

Finally, it can be said that even though some information and tools are provided voluntarily by Facebook to comply with the GDPR and provide transparency, it does not mean that a complete access to the personal information by data subjects is provided.

6.1.1.3.2 Right to Object

Facebook provides the tools to regulate privacy settings for the content provided by the users, visibility options for the content, friends and tags. Also, it is possible to manage ad preferences with the Facebook Ads tool. The tool allows users to determine whether they want to see ads based on the data provided by third parties regarding off-Facebook activities of users. As well as the ads have seen elsewhere but based on the activity data in Facebook. Furthermore, users can manage who sees the Ads which include information of their social actions in Facebook.

All these tools provide users some control over their preferences but they do not limit the data processing for profiling activities. In other words, the fact that the users may limit that Facebook won't use the data gathered from its partners about the activity off Facebook Company Products in the ads, does not mean that Facebook does not collect the personal data

---

[177] Data Policy Questions, https://www.facebook.com/help/contact/2061665240770586 (Accessed: 23.09.2019)

and process it for profiling purposes. There is no direct link(opt-out) for users to object the processing of data for direct marketing purposes or for data processing by automated means.

6.1.1.3.3 Data Retention and Right to be Forgotten

Facebook offers two ways to delete the personal data; manually on activity log and deletion of the account. If the user deleted the account, in 30 days the deletion can be retrieved, the full deletion of the data can take up to 90 days. However, even after the full deletion of the account Facebook might still hold copies of the personal data in backup storage.[178] This situation could cause a non-compliance with the GDPR regarding the right to be forgotten. However, as stated by Politou and others:[179]

> *"...applying the RtbF requirements on organizations' long-term archival storage it may not only severely affect business operations on tracking and discovering personal information within backed up and archived data, but it will also impose major challenges on advanced ERP data analytics and automated business decisions."*

Facebook specifies in the Data Policy that the deletion of an account causes only to delete the content provided directly by the user (such as photos, status updates etc.). Information provided by Facebook does not indicate the fact that the personal data collected through other partners of Facebook will be deleted too. Yet, there is a tool for requesting to erase the content provided by other users one by one under the GDPR.[180] It seems that Facebook limits the right to be forgotten only with the content users provide, not any other data collected for the data processing purposes of Facebook.

---

[178] How do I permanently delete my Facebook account?, https://www.facebook.com/help/224562897555674 (Accessed: 23.09.2019)

[179] Politou, Eugenia, Alexandra Michota, Efthimios Alepis, Matthias Pocs, and Constantinos Patsakis. "Backups and the Right to Be Forgotten in the GDPR: An Uneasy Relationship." Computer Law & Security Review: The International Journal of Technology Law and Practice 34, no. 6 (2018), p. 1256.

[180] Request Erasure of Content About Me on Facebook under GDPR, https://www.facebook.com/help/contact/812563202430607 (Accessed: 23.09.2019)

6.1.1.3.4 Right to Portability

Currently, a tool for downloading users' data is provided by Facebook. Furthermore, Facebook released a White Paper regarding data portability and the issues to be clarified.[181] In addition, there is an initiative launched in 2018 between Google, Facebook, Twitter, Microsoft and Apple to create an open-source data portability platform.[182] In spite of the fact that the right has been mentioned in the data policy, there is no information available how to exercise the right.

6.1.1.4　General Assessment

The company has taken a step forward regarding the privacy within the frame of GDPR. Especially, when the current privacy policy and settings compared with the privacy policy in 2015.[183] However, there is still a long way for the right to privacy and providing transparency. Facebook collects vast amounts of personal data and the purposes for data processing are expressed in a generic and abstract way. The users have very limited control on which data to be used by Facebook. For instance, if some sensitive data such as race, political opinion is shared in the users' profile but the settings are to seem only by the user itself, there is no limitation for Facebook to not use this data even though the privacy settings were set only for the user itself.

Even though mechanisms for consent exists, they are very limited and mostly based on opt-out procedure. Also, tools for separate consent for each data processing activity do not exist. A list for the third-parties with who the personal data shared is not provided, with the claim that Facebook does not share personal data with third-party advertisers. However, as stated above being "identifiable" is enough to be in the scope of the GDPR. As mentioned above,

---

[181] Facebook, Egan E., "Data Portability and Privacy", September 2019,
https://fbnewsroomus.files.wordpress.com/2019/09/data-portability-privacy-white-paper.pdf (Accessed: 25.09.2019)

[182] Data Transfer Project, https://datatransferproject.dev (Accessed: 23.09.2019)

[183] Alsenoy, Verdooth, Heyman, Ausloos, Wauters and Acar. *"From social media service to advertising network: A critical analysis of Facebook's Revised Policies and Terms"*, 2015. Available at:
https://www.law.kuleuven.be/citip/en/news/item/facebooks-revised-policies-and-terms-v1-3.pdf (Accessed: 21.10.2019)

even if deletion of data takes place, the situation is unclear whether the data has been kept in the back-up storage and tools for right to portability are in progress.

Accordingly, even though there is a progress regarding the privacy for users, it can be maintained that the state of the art to comply with the GDPR is not in the optimal level for Facebook.

6.1.2 Google

The privacy policy of Google (last revised January 22, 2019) is quite comprehensive but quite generic since it applies in general to different services of Google such as Search, Youtube, Google Home, Google Apps, Chrome and Android and Ads.[184] Even though the language used includes some technical terms, Google provided some links to provide some further explanations and examples. However, the privacy policy in general is spread across other documents through links, which makes it hard for the data subjects to comprehend the information necessary to be provided by the controller at a single glance.

6.1.2.1 Sources of Data, Purposes of Processing and Share of Data

Google collects a numerous amount of data on a very wide range, however the main source of data are divided into two; the data provided directly by the users and the data collected by Google as users use their services.

If a person is not signed in to a Google Account, Google uses unique identifiers[185] connected to the browser, application or device the person is using to collect and process the data. If the person is signed in to a Google Account, Google stores the data connected to this account and states that they treat the data as personal data. This approach seems problematic regarding the "identifiable data" definition of GDPR, since the data connected to the device or a browser can reveal data such as IP address, location data, phone number, which at the end might allow

---

[184] Google Privacy Policy, https://policies.google.com/privacy?hl=en-US#infocollect, (Accessed: 24.09.2019)

[185] Google defines the unique identifiers as "*a string of characters that can be used to uniquely identify a browser, app, or device. Different identifiers vary in how permanent they are, whether they can be reset by users, and how they can be accessed.*", including cookies.

the controller to identify the user by combining the data collected.[186] The language used in the privacy policy might mislead the data subjects that only the data collected through their Google account is personal data under the GDPR and, therefore benefit from the rights and protections of the GDPR for data subjects.

The types of data collected includes the data created or provided by the users such as the data given when creating the account and also the content created through usage of Google's services. Google also collects the data through the apps, browsers and devices, the activity data of users by using Google services, location information.

Apart from the data directly collected by Google, Google also collects the information available in publicly accessible sources, from marketing partners, security partners as well as advertisers. The sources to collect the data extend to use various technologies such as cookies, pixel tags, browser web storage, application data caches, databases and server logs.

Purposes of data processing are indicated as providing services, maintaining and improving the services, developing new services, providing personalised services (including content and ads), measuring performance, communicating with the users and providing security. The purposes of data processing is explained in a generic language and links to some examples are given for further explanation along with the links to privacy settings. Regarding ads, Google made it clear that the users do not receive the ads based on the sensitive data and that they do not share personal data with the advertisers without consent.[187] Even though Google indicates that they *"use automated systems that analyze your content to provide you with things like customized search results, personalized ads, or other features tailored to how you use our services"*, there is no clarification for the existence and usage of rights regulated under GDPR regarding automated decision-making and profiling. Moreover, when considered that these purposes apply to different services of Google mentioned above, they appear to be too generic and vague similar to the case of Facebook.

---

[186] Alone the IP adress accepted as personal data in the case law of ECJ. For further information see Breyer v. Germany (C-582/14).

[187] For opposite views and actions see Chapter 2.2.1.1.

Google especially specifies that they do not share the personal data with companies, organisations and individuals outside of Google.[188] Except the cases; with data subjects' consent, with the domain administrators for the services like G suite, with Google affiliated and other third parties as processors and finally for legal reasons.

6.1.2.2   Legal Basis for Processing

The legal grounds for data processing of Google consists mainly of consent of the data subjects and legitimate interests. However, in some limited cases the data processing might be based on contractual necessity or to comply with legal obligations.

The data processing of Google is primarily based on the consent of the data subjects. Google provides a tool for managing the consent settings.[189] In the settings the users can make decisions such as whether Google can collect the data for personalised Ads or voice and audio activity for speech recognition. Just like the case of Facebook, dominant position of the Google in the market must be considered when dealing with the opt-out procedures.

Google lists its legitimate interests for data processing as providing, maintaining and improving their services, developing new products, customizing services, marketing, providing advertising, providing security, performing research, fulfilling obligations to their partners and right holders and enforcing legal claims. Whether the legitimate interest overweighed by the individuals' interest or fundamental rights and freedoms must be determined on a case-by-case basis.

6.1.2.3   Data Subjects' Rights

Google provides a setting tool for controlling the activity and data collected by Google, as well as a tool called "Privacy Check-up" which provides an overview on the general privacy settings.

---

[188] Ibid.

[189] Google Account, https://myaccount.google.com/?hl=en_US (Accessed: 24.09.2019)

6.1.2.3.1 Right to be Informed

General information regarding what types of data for which purposes and on what legal grounds have been collected, with who and which data are shared are provided by Google in the Privacy Policy. However, since the data is collected through various kinds of services and aps, it could be asserted that the data provided is quite generic for a bulk of Google services. The contact information for the Google Ireland Limited (Controller in the EU, unless otherwise stated) and DPO is provided.

Regarding the right to access, access to the personal data provided by the users themselves through Google services, such as Maps, Mail, YouTube and Search, is provided in the Google Account. The users can see some data collected about them and manage their permissions for the collection of data. Even though, it is possible for data subjects to edit the data generated by themselves, the same cannot be said about the data which were collected by third-parties and connected with the users' accounts.

6.1.2.3.2 Right to Object

Google provides and opt-out for ads personalisation from Google and from partners and ad networks. Also, a plug-in for Chrome to maintain the preferences of ads personalisation is provided. Accordingly, objecting the data for direct marketing purposes is possible through Google Ads Settings.

6.1.2.3.3 Data Retention and Right to be Forgotten

Retention policy of Google is based on the types of data as some data can be deleted by the user anytime, some are deleted automatically and some data are retained for longer periods of time by Google when necessary.[190] Google keeps storing the personal data deleted by the users in an anonymised form. Personal data that users have no option to delete themselves have different retention periods and the retention period is determined depending on the data type.

---

[190] How Google Retains the Data We Collect, https://policies.google.com/technologies/retention?hl=en-US (Accessed: 25.09.2019)

Google focuses its policies more on anonymising than deleting the data permanently. Information about how Google anonymises the personal data is provided in the Data Policy.[191] There is more information provided regarding the transparency for data subjects compared to Facebook. Regarding the backups, Google states that there could be some delays for the data to be erased in the active and backup systems of Google when a user deletes the data.

6.1.2.3.4 Right to Portability

Google provides a tool for exporting the existing data to be used with a service outside of Google.[192] Also, as mentioned above the Data Transfer Project for an easier execution of data portability right between tech giants is on progress.[193]

6.1.2.4 General Assessment

The privacy policy of Google is quite generic, when it is considered that the same privacy policy applies to a multitude of services. Accordingly, a very wide range of data is collected for various purposes, which cannot be considered as "specific" under the GDPR. Separate consent mechanism for each data processing purpose is also not provided. Moreover, a unified privacy policy is not available since the pieces of information are distributed through the links for further information.

However, tools for privacy settings are provided for users to opt-out from personalised ads, as well as pausing the storing of the data regarding activities in Google services such as search data or location data. Further exercising the right to be forgotten is possible via Privacy Settings. When compared to Facebook Privacy Settings, Google's settings provide more options and control for the users regarding privacy. However, the issues regarding the dominant position of Google in the market when acquiring consent remains as well as the opt-in issues, similar to Facebook. In conclusion, even though many steps have been taken by

---

[191] How Google Anonymizes Data, https://policies.google.com/technologies/anonymization?hl=en-US (Accessed: 25.09.2019)

[192] Google Download Your Data, https://takeout.google.com/?utm_source=pp&hl=en_US&pli=1 (Accessed:23.09.2019)

[193] Data Transfer Project, https://datatransferproject.dev (Accessed: 23.09.2019)

Google regarding privacy for the data subjects, it seems that Google could improve its privacy policies.

6.2 Enforcements Against Google and Facebook in the EU

Through time there have been many privacy law violations caused by Google and Facebook. The conflict between data subjects' right to privacy and practices of these companies continues. European Union member state DPAs have brought enforcement actions against many companies for the violation of GDPR. In this section some of these cases involving Facebook and Google will be examined. The contributions of the GDPR to the right to privacy of the data subjects along with data subjects' control over their data in the context of Google and Facebook will be analysed.

6.2.1 Google

6.2.1.1 Google Ads and RTB Breach

A start-up browser maker named "Brave" recently have provided new evidence to the Irish Data Protection Commission (DPC) that Google has allegedly allowed advertising technology companies to collect and share users' personal data over 8.4 million websites. [194] Google's "DoubleClick /Authorised Buyers" ad system is based on small auctions system that take place whenever a user visits a website containing Google ads between the advertisers. Advertisers are taking place in a real-time bidding (RTB) for the data, which might include sensitive personal data.[195] Even though Google claimed that they do not serve personalised ads or send bid requests to bidders without user consent, the evidence revealed that Google allows multiple parties to match the Google identifiers for the data subject with each other via "push pages". Push pages are provided by Google to the advertisers for them to receive the same identifier for the person being profiled. The identifiers allow the advertisers to cross-

---

[194] Ryan, Johnny. "Google faces first investigation by its European lead authority for "suspected infringement" of the GDPR", following formal complaint from Brave (22.05.2019), https://brave.com/dpc-google/ (Accessed: 23.09.2019) and DPC Press Relase (22.05.2019), https://www.dataprotection.ie/en/news-media/press-releases/data-protection-commission-opens-statutory-inquiry-google-ireland-limited (Accessed: 23.09.2019)

[195] Ibid.

reference their profiles of the person, in order to trade profile data with each other. Once the data are sent, Google has no control over the data.

As mentioned in the Chapter 2.1.2, Google claims in the privacy policy that they do not share the personal data with advertisers. However, the proof indicates that they've found a worka-round to escape the privacy regulations of the GDPR regarding data subjects. This practise reveals the fact that the clash between GDPR and the practice of behavioural target adver-tisement is hard to tackle.

6.2.1.2   Google Privacy Policy Cases

In 2012, Google failed to apply the recommendations by the WP29 and comply with the privacy laws regarding it is privacy policy and practices since their policy in that time period allowed to share personal data between companies and products.[196] Accordingly, some DPAs (France, Germany, Italy, the Netherlands, Spain, and the United Kingdom) brought enforce-ment actions on the grounds that Google allowed the data transfer with 3rd parties without a valid consent of the users. [197] Commission nationale de l'informatique et des libertés (CNIL), imposed Google 150,000 Euros fine based on the lacking information provided about specific purposes of data processing, data retention periods for personal data not to exceed the period necessary for the purposes collected and information regarding consent prior to storing cookies on users' devices.[198] During the enforcement actions of Italian DPA, Google's unlawful processing of data, for behavioural advertising purposes, obtained from users' Gmail accounts was discovered.[199] It needs to be mentioned that Google's Terms of Service still states *"Our automated systems analyze your content (including emails) to provide you personally relevant product features, such as customized search results, tailored advertising, and spam and malware detection. This analysis occurs as the content is sent, received, and*

---

[196] See Letter from Article 29 Data Protection Working Party to Larry Paige, Chief Executive Officer, Google Inc. (23.09.2014) https://ec.europa.eu/justice/article-29/documentation/other-document/files/2014/20140923_letter_on_google_privacy_policy.pdf (Accessed: 27.09.2019)

[197] W. Gregory Voss, "European Union Data Privacy Law Developments", 70 Bus. Law (2014), p. 253 and 254.

[198] Whitney, L. "France Orders Google to Change Its Privacy Policies", CNET (20.06.2013), https://www.cnet.com/news/france-orders-google-to-change-its-privacy-policies/ (Accessed: 27.09.2019)

[199] Garante Per La Protezione Dei Dati Personali, "Decision Setting forth Measures Google Inc. Is Required to Take to Bring the Processing of Personal Data under Google's New Privacy Policy into Line with the Italian Data Protection Code" (10.07.2014), https://www.garanteprivacy.it/web/guest/home/docweb/-/docweb-display/docweb/3295641 (Accessed: 27.09.2019)

when it is stored." Regardless of the privacy policy changes of Google through the time, lack of transparency and problems with obtaining valid consent remains.[200]

Recently, the CNIL imposed a financial penalty of 50 Million euros against the company GOOGLE LLC, in accordance with the GDPR, for lack of transparency, inadequate information and lack of valid consent regarding the ads personalization.[201] The violations observed included that the information provided by Google is not easily accessible for users, some information is not always clear and comprehensive and most importantly violation of the obligation to have a valid consent for ads personalization processing.[202]

It is significant that regardless of the updated privacy policies of Google, the same privacy issues continues even today.[203] Google provides tools for users to create the illusion that they do have control over their data while the business model itself conflicts with the right to privacy deeply.

6.2.1.3   Right to De-reference

As previously discussed, the ECJ's judgment in Google Spain case constitutes one of the corner stones of the privacy law regarding "right to be forgotten".[204] The Court established a "right to be forgotten", meaning that on certain conditions a person can request de-reference of the links from the operator of a search engine. The case concerned a proceeding between Google Spain and Mr. Costeja regarding removal of the links concerning Mr. Costeja to third parties web pages from the list of results displayed by Google Inc. The Court did not follow the Opinion of the Advocate General in the decision.[205] The Advocate General stated that the Google could not be considered as controller since *"The internet search engine service*

---

[200] See previous privacy policies of Google: https://policies.google.com/privacy/archive?hl=en-US (Accessed: 27.09.2019) and Chapter 2.1.2.2.

[201] CNIL, "The CNIL's restricted committee imposes a financial penalty of 50 Million euros against GOOGLE LLC", (21.01.2019), https://www.cnil.fr/en/cnils-restricted-committee-imposes-financial-penalty-50-million-euros-against-google-llc (Accessed: 27.09.2019)

[202] Ibid.

[203] See Chapter 6.1.2 for privacy policy assessment of Google.

[204] Google Spain SL and Google Inc. v. Agencia Española de Protección de Datos (AEPD) and Mario Costeja González, Case C-131/12 (CJEU, 13 May 2014).

[205] Opinion of Advocate General, Google Spain SL and Google Inc. v Agencia Española de Protección de Datos (AEPD) and Mario Costeja González, C-131/12 (25.05.2013).

provider merely supplying an information location tool does not exercise control over personal data included on third-party web pages. "[206] However, the Court interpreted the term "controller" broader in its decision by stating *"It is the search engine operator which determines the purposes and means of that activity and thus of the processing of personal data that it itself carries out within the framework of that activity and which must, consequently, be regarded as the 'controller' in respect of that processing pursuant to Article 2(d). Furthermore, it would be contrary not only to the clear wording of that provision but also to its objective — which is to ensure, through a broad definition of the concept of 'controller', effective and complete protection of data subjects — to exclude the operator of a search engine from that definition on the ground that it does not exercise control over the personal data published on the web pages of third parties."*[207] It is clear that the court interpreted the term broadly to provide effective an complete protection for data subjects. However, according to the Advocate General, considering a search engine provider as "controller" would cause the service provider to *"abandon its intermediary function between the user and the publisher and assume responsibility for the content of the source web page, and when needed, to censure the content by preventing or limiting access to it."*[208]

There was also a conflict regarding the interpretation of territoriality issue, the Advocate General claimed that since the criteria of "targeted public" was not met in the case of Google Spain, territorial applicability was not possible.[209] However, the Court ruled *"...very display of personal data on a search results page constitutes processing of such data. Since that display of results is accompanied, on the same page, by the display of advertising linked to the search terms, it is clear that the processing of personal data in question is carried out in the context of the commercial and advertising activity of the controller's establishment on the territory of a Member State..."*[210]

---

[206] Ibid., para.84.

[207] Case Google Spain (C-131/12), para. 33 and 34.

[208] Opinion Google Spain (C-131/12), para. 109.

[209] Opinion Google Spain (C-131/12), para. 57.

[210] Case Google Spain (C-131/12), para. 57.

Recently, the Court made a decision regarding uncertainty of the territorial scope of de-referencing.[211] The dispute was between CNIL and Google, whether Google as a search engine operator was responsible for deploying the de-referencing to all of the domain names, when a data subject exercised the "right to de-referencing". The court admits that "...*the internet is a global network without borders and search engines render the information and links contained in a list of results displayed following a search conducted on the basis of an individual's name ubiquitous.*"[212] However, the Court stated that many third states do not recognise "right to be forgotten" along with the fact that, currently there is no obligation under EU law for a search engine operator to carry out a de-referencing on all the versions of its search engine, in case of a request made by a data subject.[213] As a result, the Court limited the responsibility of a service provider regarding territoriality of de-referencing for the all Member States of EU.[214] However, this does not mean that de-referencing on a worldwide level from the search engine operator cannot be required by the EU.[215] Especially, in the cases of providing balance between data subject's right to privacy and the protection of personal data and the right to freedom of information.

In the case *GC, AF, BH, ED v. CNIL*, the Court assessed the right to de-reference regarding sensitive data.[216] The Court ruled that a search engine operator (in this case Google) as a controller is responsible for the prohibitions and restrictions regulated under Art. 8(1) and (5) of the GDPR regarding sensitive data. However, these responsibilities and obligations apply to the search engine operators only after a de-referencing request made by the data subject and the link for sensitive data is verified under the supervision of the competent national authorities.[217] Secondly, the Court ruled that an operator of a search engine is required to weigh a request for de-referencing, between the right to be forgotten of the data subject and public interest.[218]

---

[211] Google LLC v. Commission nationale de l'informatique et des libertés (CNIL), Case C-507/17 (CJEU, 24.09.2019).

[212] Google LLC v. CNIL, Case C-507/17, para. 56.

[213] Google LLC v. CNIL, Case C-507/17, para. 64.

[214] Google LLC v. CNIL, Case C-507/17, para. 66.

[215] Google LLC v. CNIL, Case C-507/17, para. 72.

[216] GC, AF, BH, ED v. Commission nationale de l'informatique et des libertés (CNIL), Case 136/17 (CJEU, 24.09.2019).

[217] Ibid., para. 47.

[218] Ibid., para.79.

It should be noticed that the Advocate General Szpunar, followed the view of the Advocate General in Google Spain case by stating *"... if internet search engine service providers were considered [to be] controllers of the personal data on third-party source web pages and if on any of these pages there would be "special categories of data" referred to in Article 8 of ... Directive [95/46] (e.g. personal data revealing [racial or ethnic origin,] political opinions or religious [or philosophical] beliefs[, trade-union membership] or data concerning the health or sex life of individuals), the activity of the internet search engine service provider would automatically become illegal, when the stringent conditions laid down in that article for the processing of such data were not met."[219]*

The consequences and the effects of these cases to determine the scope and criteria to exercise the right to be forgotten have been major. On one hand, by applying the exercise of right to be forgotten to the modern search engine technology, the Court strengthens the hand of the data subjects. On the other hand, giving the responsibility to Google, as a controller, to censure the content when seems necessary could cause other limitations for the freedom of opinion and expression. Even though, "geo-blocking" technique creates a solution to exercise the de-referencing limited to the Europe, the Court held the possibility to apply the right worldwide as mentioned above, which could be a dangerous precedent, considering that some countries could try to censor some content they didn't like, on a global level. The risks especially for the freedom of expression cannot be undermined in such a situation. However, limiting the right to be forgotten geographically, does not give the data subjects an effective right to be forgotten, since the technology today provides many tools to go around the rules when someone is determined to access to the data in particular, such as VPN.[220] As the matter is sensitive, a good balance test and well-set criteria for the execution of the right is necessary.

---

[219] Opinion of Advocate General, GC, AF, BH, ED v. Commission nationale de l'informatique et des libertés (CNIL), Case 136/17 (10.01.2019), para. 43.

[220] Butterfield, Andrew, Gerard Ekembe Ngondi, and Anne Kerr. "VPN." A Dictionary of Computer Science, 2016, A Dictionary of Computer Science.

6.2.2   Facebook

6.2.2.1   Cambridge Analytica Data Scandal

The discovery that Facebook provided unauthorised access to the personal data of millions of peoples' individual profiles without their consent to Cambridge Analytica in 2016, has increased the privacy concerns of the individuals. Cambridge Analytica developed a profiling system called "OCEAN" profile based on; openness, conscientiousness, extraversion, agreeableness, and neuroticism) of the individuals. "OCEAN" was correlated with individuals' Facebook profile provided with the result that any personality could be analysed quite accurately.[221] Later on this "micro-targeting" allegedly used to influence the users' behaviour, for instance in the 2016 Brexit Referendum and 2016 US presidential election.[222] After the revaluation of the major data breach in March 2018 by the Guardian and New York Times, investigations took place not only in the USA but also in the EU.[223] Information Commissioner's Office (ICO) fined Facebook £500,000 for allowing application developers access to their information without sufficiently clear and informed consent.[224] Moreover, ICO fined SCL Elections, Cambridge Analytica's parent company, in January 2019 for failing to comply with an enforcement notice.[225]

As mentioned in the Chapter 6.1.1, the privacy policy of Facebook not only provides no effective tools for a valid consent, but also no enough transparency for data processing within the scope of GDPR. The Data Policy and Terms of Service are written in a so generic and vague way, the data subjects' consent is covering almost all kinds of personal data including sensitive data for further data processing such as profiling. Once Facebook acquires the

---

[221] Isaak, Jim, and Mina J Hanna. "User Data Privacy: Facebook, Cambridge Analytica, and Privacy Protection." Computer 51, no. 8 (2018), p. 57.

[222] For instance: Hern, Alex, Cambridge Analytica did work for Leave.EU, emails confirm (30.07.2019), https://www.theguardian.com/uk-news/2019/jul/30/cambridge-analytica-did-work-for-leave-eu-emails-confirm (Accessed: 27.09.2019).

[223] Cadwalladr C., Graham Harrison E., "Revealed: 50 million Facebook profiles harvested for Cambridge Analytica in major data breach" (17.03.2019), https://www.theguardian.com/news/2018/mar/17/cambridge-analytica-facebook-influence-us-election (Accessed: 23.09.2019)

[224] ICO, "ICO issues maximum £500,000 fine to Facebook for failing to protect users' personal information" (25.10.2019), https://ico.org.uk/about-the-ico/news-and-events/news-and-blogs/2018/10/facebook-issued-with-maximum-500-000-fine/ (Accessed: 24.09.2019)

[225] ICO, "SCL Elections prosecuted for failing to comply with enforcement notice" (9.01.2019), https://ico.org.uk/about-the-ico/news-and-events/news-and-blogs/2019/01/scl-elections-prosecuted-for-failing-to-comply-with-enforcement-notice/ (Accessed: 23.09.2019)

personal data, the control of the data subject is very limited on the data. Apart from the unlawful obtaining the personal data, Cambridge Analytica scandal revealed that Facebook abuses the data by using it to manipulate the individuals when their one of the basic fundamental rights at stake, freedom of choice. At that state, the consequences of the unlawful data processing violating the fundamental rights of individuals, imposing punitive fines within the scope of the GDPR, seems like a small price for Facebook to pay. Thus, preventive measures would be much effective regarding the protection of data subjects.[226]

The right to access regulated under the GDPR covers the outcomes of the processing personal data.[227] In other words, the data subjects are left in the dark regarding the profiles created about them as a result of the processing. However, after the Cambridge Analytica scandal, Facebook created a tool called "Clear History", which allows the users to see summary of their off-Facebook activity including the sources that sent your data to Facebook, and to disconnect the browsing history data from the Facebook profile.[228] "Disconnecting" does not mean deletion of the data from Facebook's servers but anonymisation of data. Even though, it is a small step towards transparency, at least there is a progress regarding the data subjects' control over their data.

6.2.2.2 Cookies Cases

In 2017, France's Data Protection Authority fined Facebook 150.000 Euros for violating the French Data Protection Act by collecting personal data through cookies without adequately informing the users.[229] Later on, some other investigations were conducted by the Netherlands, Spain, Belgium and Germany regarding the violations of privacy laws by tracking the users and non-users to use the collected data on behavioural advertising.[230] The enforcements by Spanish and Dutch DPAs followed CNIL and they fined Facebook for violating privacy

---

[226] The recent Schrems case could be an important tool providing effective preventive measures. For more information see Chapter 2.2.2.3.

[227] See Chapter 3.3.1 for more information.

[228] Facebook, F8 2018 Keynote, https://www.youtube.com/watch?v=ldtuSYqgPLQ , (Accessed: 04.10.2019)

[229] CNIL, "Facebook sanctioned for several breaches of the French Data Protection Act" (16.052017), http://www.globalsecuritymag.fr/FACEBOOK-sanctioned-for-several,20170516,71112.html (Accessed: 28.09.2019)

[230] Gibbs, Samuel, "Facebook facing privacy actions across Europe as France fines firm €150k" (16.06.2017), https://www.theguardian.com/technology/2017/may/16/facebook-facing-privacy-actions-across-europe-as-france-fines-firm-150k (Accessed: 28.09.2019)

laws.[231] Belgian court ordered Facebook to terminate violating the privacy laws by unlawfully tracking individuals on third-party websites in February 2018. In the same month, German regional court in Berlin found the data usage by Facebook illegal on the grounds of lacking legitimate consent and pre-checked opt-in boxes.[232]

During these procedures, Facebook claimed that other European DPAs had no jurisdiction since the subsidiary of Facebook is located in Ireland. However, ECJ ruling indicates the opposite in the case *Wirtschaftsakademie.*[233] Finally, the consent of the data subjects is integral part of data processing when there is no application of other legal basis regulated under the GDPR.[234] Therefore, it is essential that the companies respect and apply the regulations outlined in the GDPR for data processing to be lawful. Online and offline tracking activities of Facebook take place without a valid consent of the data subjects, infringing the rights of the data subjects.

6.2.2.3   Schrems (Safe Harbour Case) and Schrems 2.0

As previously discussed, Facebook is an American tech company, which has establishments outside the EU.[235] Meaning the fact that the data collected from European citizens is not just stored within the EU. An Austrian student named Maximilian Schrems claimed that the US based company Facebook transferred personal data of the European citizens through its subsidiary Facebook Ireland and that the receiving country(US) did not provide adequate level of protection.[236] The argument used for US providing no adequate level of protection

---

[231] Hetz, R., Binnie, Isla, "Facebook Fined 1.2Million Euros by Spanish Data Watchdog", (11.09.2017
https://www.reuters.com/article/us-facebook-spain-fine/facebook-fined-1-2-million-euros-by-spanish-data-watchdog-idUSKCN1BM1OU (Accessed: 29.09.2019) and Dutch Data Protection Authority: Facebook Violates Privacy Law (23.02.2017),
https://autoriteitpersoonsgegevens.nl/sites/default/files/atoms/files/conclusions_facebook_february_23_2017.pdf (Accessed: 29.09.2019)

[232] Landgericht Berlin, (16.01.2018),
https://www.vzbv.de/sites/default/files/downloads/2018/02/12/facebook_lg_berlin.pdf
(Accessed:28.09.2019)

[233] Unabhängiges Landeszentrum für Datenschutz Schleswig- Holstein v. Wirtschaftsakademie Schleswig-Holstein GmbH, C-210/16, (CJEU, 5.6.2018), para. 52.

[234] See Chapter 3.2.1 for more information.

[235] See Chapter 2.1 for more information.

[236] Maximillian Schrems v. Data Protection Commissioner, C-361/14 (CJEU, 06.10.2019)

was based on the unlawful accessing to personal data revealed by Snowden.[237] Based on the facts, ECJ invalidated the Safe Harbour agreement between Europe and US.[238] ECJ stated that *"legislation not providing for any possibility for an individual to pursue legal remedies in order to have access to personal data relating to him, or to obtain the rectification or erasure of such data, does not respect the essence of the fundamental right to effective judicial protection".[239]*

Currently another application made by Schrems is in process regarding the current standard contractual clauses (SCC) of the European Commission.[240] This case concerns not only the data transfers to the US but all cross-border data transfers. Since the SCC are the most commonly used mechanism used in practise to legitimate data transfers to non-EU counties, the decision of the Court will be crucial for data transfers to third countries. The validity of U.S Privacy Shield might be impacted by the decision as well as the businesses of Google and Facebook since their activities of cross-border data transfers are currently based on the SSCs. If the Court rules that SSCs do not adequately meet the data protection laws of the EU, the data transfers between the EU and US could come to a full stop.

---

[237] For more information regarding the Snowden revelations see: https://www.theguardian.com/us-news/the-nsa-files

[238] CJEU, "Press Release No 117/15, The Court of Justice declares that the Commission's US Safe Harbour Decision is invalid", http://www.politico.eu/wp-content/uploads/2015/10/schrems-judgment.pdf (Accessed:29.09.2019)

[239] Schrems v. Data Commissioner, para. 95.

[240] Application Schrems v. Data Protection Commissioner, C-311/18 (CJEU, 9.5.2019)

7 Conclusion

One of the primary aims of the GDPR is to increase the participation of data subjects and to grant them more control over their data. In that regard, the compliance of the companies is crucial for the realization of the aims of the GDPR. Since Google and Facebook are global companies collecting and processing vast amounts of personal data, their compliance with the GDPR is essential to ensure better protection of the data subjects.

Within that framework, this work aimed to answer the question, whether Google and Facebook comply with the GDPR sufficiently regarding data subjects' rights and whether an adequate level of control over their data is provided. Current privacy policies (both cookies and general privacy policies) of these companies have been analysed to determine whether they fulfill their duties to inform the data subjects about data processing with respect to the general principles of the GDPR. The general outcome of the analyses indicates that the privacy policies of both of the companies tend to be generic and abstract and are therefore problematic regarding the principle of transparency of the GDPR. In addition to that, specific and limited purposes of data processing are not provided and specific consent for each purpose is not obtained by Google and Facebook. The Cambridge Analytica scandal has demonstrated not only how important it is for the protection of data subjects to provide transparency, but also what severe effects processing vast amounts of data unlawfully can have for the right to privacy.

Furthermore, one of the most serious issues observed was the negligence of the duties specified GDPR when obtaining valid consent of the data subjects for processing data. Consent of data subjects needs to be freely given, informed, specific and unambiguous in order to be valid. However, the clear imbalance between the companies and data subjects affects the validity of the consent since the criteria "freely given" is not provided. Moreover, regarding the criteria "specific" the terms of service and privacy policies of both Google and Facebook require the consent of the users for bundled services and subsidiaries. Even though some tools are provided for opt-out from specific data collections, the companies keep collecting user-generated data online and off-line. Not only privacy the policies are insufficient for obtaining valid consent of the users but also the activities of the companies are violating the GDPR, including sharing personal data with third parties without valid consent of the data subjects as in the case of Google Ads and Facebook cookies.

Facebook and Google have been taking steps to provide more tools for the users so that they are able to control their data better and comply with the GDPR. However, the tools, companies provide for data subjects to exercise their rights, are found to be superficial. For instance, regarding the right to access the data, the companies provide only access to the activity history of users even though they also collect data through offline activities of the users and the data generated off-Google and Facebook accounts are used for profiling and targeted advertising activities within Google and Facebook. Also, the right to object for direct advertising can be exercised through ad settings services of Facebook and Google. However, the tool Facebook provides only offers preference management regarding advertisements. Thus, the tool does not limit the data processing of Facebook for profiling and targeted advertising services.

Whether an adequate level of protection is provided regarding cross-border data transfers is still open to debate as mentioned in the Schrems case. In addition to that, the recent *Google* decision of the CJEU regarding the right to be forgotten is expected to have major effects regarding the exercise of the right, since the territorial limitation of the right with the EU does not match the global and open nature of the internet. However, the concerns of the Court regarding freedom of opinion is understandable.

Essentially, the "take-it-or-leave-it" approach of Google and Facebook based on their dominant position in the online market remains. In spite of the fact that they do provide some tools for complying with the GDPR and data subjects to exercise their rights, the tools do not allow users to exercise their rights fully or control the data collected about them efficiently.

Finally, to answer the main research question of this work, the findings demonstrate that the theoretical level regulated under the GDPR regarding data subjects' rights and their control over the data does not correspond with the practices of the Google and Facebook in general, and even if they do it takes place in a very limited manner. Complying with the principle of transparency, acquiring valid consent to process the data and also to sharing the data with third parties for advertising seems to be the most problematic issues.

Table of reference

Treaties/Statutes

- Commission Decision 2000/520/EC of 26 July 2000 pursuant to Directive 95/46/EC of the European Parliament and of the Council on the adequacy of the protection provided by the safe harbour privacy principles and related frequently asked questions issued by the US Department of Commerce, OJ L 215.
- Commission Implementing Decision (EU) 2016/1250 of 12 July 2016 pursuant to Directive 95/46/EC of the European Parliament and of the Council on the adequacy of the protection provided by the EU-U.S. Privacy Shield
- Convention for the Protection of Individuals with regard to Automatic Processing of Personal Data (Council of Europe) and the Convention as amended by Protocol CETS No. 223.Directive 2002/58/EC of the European Parliament and of the Council of 12 July 2002 concerning the processing of personal data and the protection of privacy in the electronic communications sector (Directive on privacy and electronic communications) as amended by Directive 2006/24/EC and Directive 2009/136/EC.
- Directive 95/46/EC of the European Parliament and of the Council of 24 Oct. 1995 On the protection of individuals with regard to the processing of personal data and on the free movement of such data, OJ L 281, 23 Nov. 1995.
- OECD Guidelines on data protection (2013) – Guidelines Governing the Protection of Privacy and Trans-border Flows of Personal Data, (Adopted 23.9.1980). Available at: http://www.oecd.org/sti/ieconomy/2013-oecd-privacy-guidelines.pdf
- Privacy Shield Framework, https://www.privacyshield.gov/welcome (Accessed: 29.09.2019)
- Proposal for a Regulation of the European Parliament and of the Council concerning the respect for private life and the protection of personal data in electronic communications and repealing Directive 2002/58/EC (Regulation on Privacy and Electronic Communications), Brussels, 10.1.2017, 2017/0003(COD).
- Regulation (Eu) 2016/679 of the European Parliament and of the Council on the Protection of Natural Persons with Regard to the Processing of Personal Data and on the Free Movement of Such Data, and Repealing Directive 95/46/Ec (General Data Protection Regulation), OJ L. 119/1, 4.5.2016."

Books, Articles and Journals

- Alsenoy, Verdooth, Heyman, Ausloos, Wauters and Acar. From social media service to advertising network: A critical analysis of Facebook's Revised Policies and Terms, 2015. Available at: https://www.law.kuleuven.be/citip/en/news/item/facebooks-revised-policies-and-terms-v1-3.pdf (Accessed: 21.09.2019)
- Boerman, Sophie C, Sanne Kruikemeier, and Frederik J Zuiderveen Borgesius. "Online Behavioral Advertising: A Literature Review and Research Agenda." Journal of Advertising 46, no. 3 (2017): 363-76., DOI: 10.1080/00913367.2017.1339368.
- Butterfield, Andrew, Gerard Ekembe Ngondi, and Anne Kerr. "VPN." A Dictionary of Computer Science, 2016, A Dictionary of Computer Science. eISBN: 9780191768125.
- Bygrave, L.A. "Data Protection Law: Approaching Its Rationale, Logic and Limits." Journal of Information, Law & Technology 1 (2002): Journal of Information, Law & Technology, 2002, Vol.1
- Bygrave, Lee A. Data Privacy Law: An International Perspective. Oxford: Oxford University Press, 2014.
- Cuevas, Ángel, Cabañas, José González, Arrate, Aritz, and Cuevas, Rubén. "Does Facebook Use Sensitive Data for Advertising Purposes? Worldwide Analysis and GDPR Impact." 2019.
- De Hert, Papakonstantinou, Malgieri, Beslay, and Sanchez. "The Right to Data Portability in the GDPR: Towards User-centric Interoperability of Digital Services." Com- puter Law & Security Review: The International Journal of Technology Law and Prac- tice 34, no. 2, 2018: 193-203.
- Doyle, Charles. "Real-time Bidding." A Dictionary of Marketing, 2016.
- Dreyer,S., Schulz W. , "The General Data Protection Regulation and Automated Decision-making: Will it deliver?", BertelsmannStiftung (2019), https://www.bertelsmann-stiftung.de/fileadmin/files/BSt/Publikationen/GrauePublikationen/GDPR.pdf (Acces- sed: 28.09.2019)
- European Union Agency for Fundamental Rights and Council of Europe, "Handbook on European data protection law", 201s.
- Gribing Arlfors, Christian, and Simon Nilsson. "Tracking the Cookies: A Quantitative Study on User Perceptions about Online Tracking." 2019.

- Helena Ursic. "Unfolding the New-Born Right to Data Portability: Four Gateways to Data Subject Control." SCRIPTed: A Journal of Law, Technology & Society 15, no. 1 (2018): 42-69.

- Hildebrandt, Mireille, and Serge Gutwirth. Profiling the European Citizen: Cross- disiplinary Perspectives. S.l.: Springer, 2008.

- Isaak, Jim, and Mina J Hanna. "User Data Privacy: Facebook, Cambridge Analytica, and Privacy Protection." Computer 51, no. 8 (2018): 56-59.

- Kamlah, W. (2016). In K. U. Plath (Ed.), BDSG/DSGVO Kommentar zum BDSG und zur DSGVO sowie den Datenschutzbestimmungen von TMG und TKG (2nd ed.). Cologne: Otto Schmidt.

- Kristol, David. "HTTP Cookies: Standards, Privacy, and Politics." ACM Transactions on Internet Technology (TOIT) 1, no. 2 (2001): 151-98.

- Maris, Elena, Timothy Libert, and Jennifer Henrichsen. "Tracking Sex: The Implica- tions of Widespread Sexual Data Leakage and Tracking on Porn Websites." 2019.

- Martini, M. (2018). In B. Paal & D. A. Pauly (Eds.), Datenschutz-Grundverordnung Bundesdatenschutzgesetz (2nd ed.). Munich: C.H. Beck.

- Martini, M. (2018). In B. Paal & D. A. Pauly (Eds.), Datenschutz-Grundverordnung Bundesdatenschutzgesetz (2nd ed.). Munich: C.H. Beck.

- McDonald, Aleecia M., & Cranor, Lorrie Faith. (2009). An Empirical Study of How People Perceive Online Behavioral Advertising. CMU-CyLab-09-015. Retrieved from https://www.cylab.cmu.edu/_files/pdfs/tech_reports/CMUCyLab09015.pdf, Last Accessed: 14.08.2019.

- ning", (2018) http://www3.weforum.org/docs/WEF_40065_White_Paper_How_to_Prevent_Discriminatory_Outcomes_in_Machine_Learning.pdf (Accessed: 20.09.2019)

- Politou, Eugenia, Alexandra Michota, Efthimios Alepis, Matthias Pocs, and Constantinos Patsakis. "Backups and the Right to Be Forgotten in the GDPR: An Uneasy Relationship." Computer Law & Security Review: The International Journal of Technology Law and Practice 34, no. 6, 2018: 1247-257.

- Reins, Leonie. Regulating New Technologies in Uncertain Times. Vol. 32. Information Technology and Law Series. The Hague, 2019.

- Rouvroy, Antoinette, and Yves Poullet. "The Right to Informational Self-determination and the Value of Self-development. Reassessing the Importance of Privacy for Democracy." In Reinventing Data Protection?, 2009.
- Rustici, Chiara. "GDPR Profiling and Business Practice." Computer Law Review International 19, no. 2 (2018): 34-43.
- Schulz, S. (2017). In P. Gola (Ed.), Datenschutz-Grundverordnung VO (EU) 2016/679 Kommentar. Munich: C.H. Beck
- Smith, H. Jeff, Information Privacy and its Management," MIS Quarterly Executive: Vol. 3: Issue 4, Article 6, 2008. Available at: https://aisel.aisnet.org/misqe/vol3/iss4/6
- Spahiu, Irma. "Google Spain and Google." European Public Law 21, no. 4 (2015): 691-702.
- Steppe, Richard. "Online Price Discrimination and Personal Data: A General Data Protection Regulation Perspective." Computer Law & Security Review: The International Journal of Technology Law and Practice 33, no. 6 2017.
- Tene, Omer, and Polonetsky, Jules. "To Track or "do Not Track": Advancing Transparency and Individual Control in Online Behavioral Advertising." Minnesota Journal of Law, Science & Technology 13, no. 1 (2012): 281-357.
- W. Gregory Voss, European Union Data Privacy Law Developments, 70 Bus. Law (2014).
- Wong, Rebecca. "Social Networking: A Conceptual Analysis of a Data Controller." Communications Law 14, no. 5 (2009): 142-49.
- World Economic Forum "How to Prevent Discriminatory Outcomes in Machine Lear-
- Zednik C., "Solving the Black Box Problem: A General-Purpose Recipe for Explainable Artificial Intelligence", 2019.

Opinions and Reports

- Article 29 Data Protection Working Party, Guidelines on Automated individual decision-making and Profiling for the purposes of Regulation 2016/679, WP251rev.01, 06.02.2018.
- Article 29 Working Party (2016), Guidelines on the right to data portability, WP 242, 13 December 2016 and revised on 5 April 2017.
- Article 29 Working Party, Guidelines on consent under Regulation 2016/679, WP259 rev.01, Brussels, 10.04.2018.
- Article 29 Working Party, Opinion 03/2013 on Purpose Limitation, Brussels, 02.04.2013

- Article 29 Working Party, Opinion 06/2014 on the Notion of legitimate interests of the data controller under Article 7 of Directive 95/46/EC, 09.04.2014.

- Council of Europe, Explanatory Report to the Protocol amending the Convention for the Protection of Individuals with regard to Automatic Processing of Personal Data, No.223, 10.10.2018

- EDPB, EU - U.S. Privacy Shield - Second Annual Joint Review, 22. 01.2019.

- EDPB, Guidelines 3/2018 on the territorial scope of the GDPR (Article 3) - Version for public consultation, 16.10.2018.

- EDPB, Opinion 5/2019 on the interplay between the ePrivacy Directive and the GDPR, in particular regarding the competence, tasks and powers of data protection authorities, 12.03.2019.

- European Commission, "Special Eurobarometer 487a Report", GDPR, (June 2019).

- European Commission, Report from The Commission To The European Parliament And The Council on the second annual review of the functioning of the EU-U.S. Privacy Shield, Brussels, 19.12.2018.

- United States Securities and and Exchange Comission, Form 10-Q, "Quarterly Report of Facebook, Inc." (For the quarterly period ended 31.03.2019), Available at: https://www.sec.gov/Archives/edgar/data/1326801/000132680119000037/fb-03312019x10q.htm. (Accessed: 11.09.2019)

- United States Securities and Exchange Commisison Form 10-K, "Annual Report of Facebook, Inc." (For the fiscal year ended 31.12.2018) Available at: https://www.sec.gov/Archives/edgar/data/1326801/000132680119000009/fb-12312018x10k.htm (Accessed: 11.09.2019)

- United States Securities and Exchange Commission, Form 10-Q, "Annual Report of Alphabet Inc." (For the fiscal year ended 31.12.2018). Available at: https://www.sec.gov/Archives/edgar/data/1652044/000165204419000004/goog10-kq42018.htm#s6C1DB95EDB3C5C7998B5E96D339C677B (Accessed: 11.09.2019)

Case Law

- Application Schrems v. Data Protection Commissioner, C-311/18 (CJEU, 9 May 2019)
- Asociación Nacional de Establecimientos Financieros de Crédito (ASNEF) and Federación de Comercio Electrónico y Marketing Directo (FECEMD) v. Administración del Estado, Joined cases C-468/10 and C-469/10 (CJEU, 25 November 2011)
- British Gas Trading Limited Vs. The Data Protection Register.
- BVerfGE 65, 1 – Volkszählung Urteil des Ersten Senats vom 15. Dezember 1983 auf die mündliche Verhandlung vom 18. und 19. Oktober 1983 – 1 BvR 209, 269, 362, 420, 440, 484/83 in den Verfahren über die Verfassungsbeschwerden. (15 December 1983)
- CJEU, La Quadrature du Net and Others v Commission, T-738/16, (Action brought on 25 October 2016.)
- Facebook, Exploitative business terms pursuant to Section 19(1) GWB for inadequate data processing, Bundeskartelamt (B6-22/16), 06 February 2019.
- Fashion ID GmbH & Co. KG v. Verbraucherzentrale NRW eV, C-40/17 (CJEU, 29 July 2019)
- Google LLC v. Commission nationale de l'informatique et des libertés (CNIL), Case C-507/17 (CJEU, 24 September 2019)
- Google Spain SL and Google Inc. v. Agencia Española de Protección de Datos (AEPD) and Mario Costeja González, Case C-131/12 (CJEU, 13 May 2014)
- Google Spain SL, Google Inc. v. Agencia Española de Protección de Datos (AEPD), Mario Costeja González [GC], C-131/12 (CJEU, 13 May 2014)
- Google Spain SL, Google Inc. v. Agencia Española de Protección de Datos (AEPD), Mario Costeja González, C-131/12 (CJEU, 13 May 2014)
- Heinz Huber v. Bundesrepublik Deutschland [GC], C-524/06 (CJEU, 16 December 2008)
- Joined cases Digital Rights Ireland Ltd v. Minister for Communications, Marine and Natural Resources and Others and Kärntner Landesregierung and Others, C-293/12 and C-594/12, (CJEU, 8 April 2014).
- Joined Cases Tele2 Sverige AB v. Postoch telestyrelsen, and Secretary of State for the Home Department, C-203/15 and C-698/15, (CJEU, 21. December 2016)
- K.H. and Others v. Slovakia No. 32881/04, (ECtHR, 28 April 2009)
- Maximillian Schrems v. Data Protection Commissioner, C-361/14 (CJEU, 06 October 2019)

- Opinion of Advocate General, Google Spain SL and Google Inc. v Agencia Española de Protección de Datos (AEPD) and Mario Costeja González, C-131/12 (25 May 2013).
- Planet49 GmbH v. Bundesverband der Verbraucherzentralen und Verbraucherverbände – Verbraucherzentrale Bundesverband e.V. (C-673/17), Opinion of Advocate General, 21 March 2019.
- Planet49 GmbH v. Bundesverband der Verbraucherzentralen und Verbraucherverbände – Verbraucherzentrale Bundesverband e.V., C-673/17, (CJEU, 01 October 2019).
- Rechnungshof v. Österreichischer Rundfunk and Others and Christa Neukomm and Jospeh Lauermann v. Österreichischer Rundfunk, Joined cases C-465/00, C-138/01 and C-139/01 (CJEU, 20 May 2003)
- S. And Marper V. The United Kingdom, No. 30562/04 30566/04.
- Unabhängiges Landeszentrum für Datenschutz Schleswig- Holstein v. Wirtschaftsakademie Schleswig-Holstein GmbH, C-210/16, (CJEU, 5 June 2018).
- Unabhängiges Landeszentrum für Datenschutz Schleswig-Holstein v. Wirtschaftsakademie Schleswig-Holstein GmbH, C-210/16 (CJEU, 5 June 2018)
- Weltimmo s. r. o. v. Nemzeti Adatvédelmi és Információszabadság Hatóság, C-230/14, (CJEU, 1 October 2015)

Other Sources

- Cadwalladr C., Graham Harrison E., Revealed: 50 million Facebook profiles harvested for Cambridge Analytica in major data breach (17.03.2019), https://www.theguardian.com/news/2018/mar/17/cambridge-analytica-facebook-influence-us-election (Accessed: 23.09.2019)
- Chromium Blog, Improving Privacy and Security on the Web, 07.05.2019. Available at: https://blog.chromium.org/2019/05/improving-privacy-and-security-on-web.html (Accessed: 04.09.2019)
- Chromium Blog, Improving Privacy and Security on the Web, 07.05.2019. Available at: https://blog.chromium.org/2019/05/improving-privacy-and-security-on-web.html (Accessed: 04.09.2019)
- CJEU, Press Release No 117/15, The Court of Justice declares that the Commission's US Safe Harbour Decision is invalid, http://www.politico.eu/wp-content/uploads/2015/10/schrems-judgment.pdf (Accessed:29.09.2019)

- CNIL, Facebook sanctioned for several breaches of the French Data Protection Act (16.052017), http://www.globalsecuritymag.fr/FACEBOOK-sanctioned-for-several,20170516,71112.html (Accessed: 28.09.2019)
- Data Policy Questions, https://www.facebook.com/help/contact/2061665240770586 (Accessed: 23.09.2019)
- Data Protection Commission Ireland, https://www.dataprotection.ie/en/news-media/press-releases/data-protection-commission-opens-statutory-inquiry-google-ireland-limited (Accessed: 23.09.2019)
- Data Transfer Project, https://datatransferproject.dev (Accessed: 23.09.2019)
- Dutch Data Protection Authority: Facebook Violates Privacy Law (23.02.2017), https://autoriteitpersoonsgegevens.nl/sites/default/files/atoms/files/conclusions_facebook_february_23_2017.pdf (Accessed: 29.09.2019)
- Facebook Data Policy, https://www.facebook.com/policy.php (Accessed: 19.09.2019)
- Facebook Privacy Legal Bases, https://www.facebook.com/about/privacy/legal_bases (Accessed: 20.09.2019)
- Facebook Terms of Service, https://www.facebook.com/legal/terms/update (Accessed: 20.09.2019)
- Facebook, Cookies & Other Storage Technologies. Available at: https://www.facebook.com/policy/cookies/ (Accessed: 04.09.2019)
- Facebook, Egan E., Data Portability and Privacy, September 2019, https://fbnewsroomus.files.wordpress.com/2019/09/data-portability-privacy-white-paper.pdf (Accessed: 25.09.2019)
- Facebook, F8 2018 Keynote, https://www.youtube.com/watch?v=ldtuSYqgPLQ , (Accessed: 04.10.2019)
- Garante Per La Protezione Dei Dati Personali, Decision Setting forth Measures Google Inc. Is Required to Take to Bring the Processing of Personal Data under Google´s New Privacy Policy into Line with the Italian Data Protection Code (10.07.2014), https://www.garanteprivacy.it/web/guest/home/docweb/-/docweb-display/docweb/3295641 (Accessed: 27.09.2019)
- Gibbs, Samuel, Facebook facing privacy actions across Europe as France fines firm €150k (16.06.2017), https://www.theguardian.com/technology/2017/may/16/facebook-facing-privacy-actions-across-europe-as-france-fines-firm-150k (Accessed: 28.09.2019)
- Google Account, https://myaccount.google.com/?hl=en_US (Accessed: 24.09.2019)

- Google Analytics Cookie Usage on Websites. Available at: https://developers.google.com/analytics/devguides/collection/analyticsjs/cookie-usage (Accessed: 04.09.2019) and Alphabet Cookie Policy. Available at: https://www.alphabet.com/en-ww/cookies (Accessed: 04.09.2019)

- Google Download Your Data, https://takeout.google.com/?utm_source=pp&hl=en_US&pli=1 (Accessed:23.09.2019)

- Google Privacy Policy, https://policies.google.com/privacy?hl=en-US#infocollect, (Accessed: 24.09.2019)

- Google, 2019, Cookie Policy. [Online] Available at: https://policies.google.com/technologies/cookies?hl=en-US (Accessed: 03.09.2019)

- Hern, Alex, Cambridge Analytica did work for Leave.EU, emails confirm (30.07.2019), https://www.theguardian.com/uk-news/2019/jul/30/cambridge-analytica-did-work-for-leave-eu-emails-confirm (Accessed: 27.09.2019).

- Hetz, R., Binnie, Isla, Facebook Fined 1.2Million Euros by Spanish Data Watchdog, REUTERS (11.09.2017 https://www.reuters.com/article/us-facebook-spain-fine/facebook-fined-1-2-million-euros-by-spanish-data-watchdog-idUSKCN1BM1OU (Accessed: 29.09.2019)

- How do I permanently delete my Facebook account?, https://www.facebook.com/help/224562897555674 (Accessed: 23.09.2019)

- How Google Anonymizes Data, https://policies.google.com/technologies/anonymization?hl=en-US (Accessed: 25.09.2019)

- How Google Retains the Data We Collect, https://policies.google.com/technologies/retention?hl=en-US (Accessed: 25.09.2019)

- ICO, ICO issues maximum £500,000 fine to Facebook for failing to protect users' personal information (25.10.2019), https://ico.org.uk/about-the-ico/news-and-events/news-and-blogs/2018/10/facebook-issued-with-maximum-500-000-fine/ (Accessed: 24.09.2019)

- ICO, SCL Elections prosecuted for failing to comply with enforcement notice (9.01.2019), https://ico.org.uk/about-the-ico/news-and-events/news-and-blogs/2019/01/scl-elections-prosecuted-for-failing-to-comply-with-enforcement-notice/ (Accessed: 23.09.2019)

- Instagram, About Cookies. Available at: https://help.instagram.com/1896641480634370?ref=ig (Accessed: 04.09.2019)

- Landgericht Berlin, (16.01.2018), https://www.vzbv.de/sites/default/files/downloads/2018/02/12/facebook_lg_berlin.pdf (Accessed:28.09.2019)

- Previous Privacy Policies of Google: https://policies.google.com/privacy/archive?hl=en-US (Accessed: 27.09.2019)

- Request Erasure of Content About Me on Facebook under GDPR, https://www.facebook.com/help/contact/812563202430607 (Accessed: 23.09.2019)

- Ryan, Johnny. Google faces first investigation by its European lead authority for "suspected infringement" of the GDPR, following formal complaint from Brave (22.05.2019), https://brave.com/dpc-google/ (Accessed: 23.09.2019)

- See Letter from Article 29 Data Protection Working Party to Larry Paige, Chief Executive Officer, Google Inc. (23.09.2014) https://ec.europa.eu/justice/article-29/documentation/other-document/files/2014/20140923_letter_on_google_privacy_policy.pdf (Accessed: 27.09.2019)

- Statcounter Netmarketshare. Search Engine Market Share United States of America, 2019. Available at: http://gs.statcounter.com (Accessed: 04.09.2019)

- WhatsApp Legal Info. Available at: https://www.whatsapp.com/legal/ (Accessed: 04.09.2019)

- Whitney, L. France Orders Google to Change Its Privacy Policies, CNET (20.06.2013), https://www.cnet.com/news/france-orders-google-to-change-its-privacy-policies/ (Accessed: 27.09.2019)